Of Boys, Men and Mountains

Of Boys, Men and Mountains

ROY TOMKINSON

The book is dedicated to
My Grandparents,
Parents,
Mog

ISBN: 0 86243 868 3

cover: 'Miners' by Don Owen

Dinas is an imprint of Y Lolfa

Printed and published in Wales
by Y Lolfa Cyf., Talybont, Ceredigion SA24 5AP
e-mail ylolfa@ylolfa.com
website www.ylolfa.com
tel. (01970) 832304
fax (01970) 832782

Chapter 1

I WAS BORN ON A WARM, sunny day, so my mother told me, in a small place called Cwmparc, in the Rhondda Valley. Many stories and songs have been written about the Rhondda, and even today it is still a place that stirs people's emotions, some good and some bad. People born in the Valley share a sense of belonging, but also a feeling of contempt for still living there. Those that have moved on have a feeling of: *I am glad I was there.* The song, *if I could see the Rhondda one more time,* creates a feeling of warmth and pride in the people born in the Rhondda Valley.

They say you can run but not hide. You can pretend that things were different, but when you were born and bred in the Valley, to reject this, is to reject your very existence. Valley blood stays in the veins until you die. Rhondda people are proud of their heritage; they are hard, proud people, forged from coal, and tempered by Chapel and Church every Sunday.

I have not always understood this sense of pride, and, in my early years, I rejected a lot of the values instilled into me by the environment into which I was born. I wanted better than this, and I felt that Valley people had no ambition or pride, but accepted what life threw at them. I see now that it was the Rhondda and its people that forged my personality. The values I have come from my parents. It was the Rhondda that was too good for me. Until I realised this, there could be no growth.

Before the coalmines came, the Valley was covered in trees, with a river running the length of the valley floor. They say it was possible for a squirrel to jump from one tree to another and not touch the ground until it reached Cardiff. The population was only a few dozen, at the most, working as farmers and in harmony with an environment that had not changed in centuries. When Black Gold was found beneath the ground, in less than a decade, the landscape changed permanently.

My first recollection of my birthplace is of mountains, not trees, but black mountains, dusty, dirty, and grey to the look and feel, everything monochrome, no green, and no bright warm colours, nothing to warm the soul. Dirt was everywhere, in the house, on the roof, ingrained and etched into the faces of the people. Black and white, white and black, grey and grey, dark and dark, dust and dust: hopelessness, despair, a sense of existing not living, this was the Valley into which I was born.

There were endless rows of small terraced houses, sloping slate roofs, all identical. It was like a huge patchwork quilt without the colour. Each house had been squeezed into an area too small to give it dignity, yet its inhabitants were not lacking in pride. Most front doors were painted a similar colour, a nondescript type of dark grey, unappealing but adequate. Any other colour would have seemed out of place. The windows reflected this air of despondency. The houses, row upon row, and line upon line, were functional and adequate, just, for the job.

This is the Rhondda I remember; picturesque it was not. The landscape was scarred by tip waste, hacked from the bowels of the earth by men who often paid with their lives for the coal they mined. A scar on the landscape is not the landscape itself, and to find the beauty, one has to look beneath the dirt and degradation, which are but skin deep. There is depth, strength, power and beauty in the soil from which we all came and to which we shall return, when our life is over.

The same deep, proud beauty, forged on the anvils of the Valley, and in the generations that have gone before and are long since dead, can be seen in the people of the Rhondda, if we look deeply into their character. Black Gold, then, takes on a whole new meaning. The heart of the Rhondda lies in its people.

This is the Rhondda I could not see because I was too concerned in getting out. I wanted to conquer the world. I blamed my upbringing for everything that went wrong. I was angry, vengeful, wanted what other people had, and blamed everyone except the right person for what I lacked. All the time, the answer was under my very nose: *the blame was mine.*

A Greek sage once said, "Know thyself." This means, know what you are and take responsibility for your own destiny. Acceptance brings resignation, calms the anger, and leaves you no place to go other than inside yourself, something few people experience. I feel lucky that I had this experience, and I thank my lucky stars for my Rhondda upbringing and my hardworking parents.

My father, the fathers of both parents, and my uncles were miners, or worked in the pit. We knew only the way of the colliery. The noise from the pit was constant. A loud whistle blew to start and end each shift, and there were three shifts every day. My house was next to the pit, and from my bedroom window I could see the winder lowering and raising each shift as the day progressed.

I was so used to the noise that I only noticed it when it stopped, at Christmas and during the miner's holidays. A winder in motion sounds like a drum beating to a constant rhythm, when it takes the miners from the light of day into the bowels of the earth and brings them back after their shift is over. Many times, I watched the men going into the cage, singing and smiling on their way to work. They spoke in a low kind of drone, in order to be heard above the sound of the drum. I cannot say whether they were contented with their lot, for they had no choice. If they seemed happy on the outside, inwardly, they might have been wishing that things were different.

Eldest in a family of three male children, I was born in a small terraced house at the top of Cwmparc, next to the Park Colliery

Pit. My father and mother owned the house, and this was a source of pride. They had a mortgage, but that did not matter because the house would eventually be paid for. They used to tell me that there would always be a home for me, if I ever needed a roof over my head. My father used to say this with a proud voice.

"I am here, my son, I am here. I will always be here. Call out if you need help."

It was years later, when I was wise enough to understand what he meant. My father worked at the coalface, cutting coal; the more coal he cut, the greater the bonus. He felt proud that he could earn extra money by working harder. He used to tell me that he did not always take the full food break, but worked *through* for a few extra pounds. This meant nothing to me at the time, but he instilled in me a sense of pride and commitment that I understood much later.

I remember as if it were yesterday, my father coming home from the mine, black face, smiling. I would look up to him and see love in his eyes. I can feel that love, even now; I can see his face looking at me. He is still in my heart and he will stay there until he comes to collect me, when my journey in this life is over. I would not part with these memories; they are more precious to me than I can describe.

Once every three weeks, my father would work a day shift, from six in the morning until mid afternoon. He preferred this early morning shift to the others because he could spend the rest of the day in the garden. When on holiday from school, I would wait at the back door, next to our outdoor toilet at the bottom of the garden, for my father to appear. I knew the exact time he would come into sight. The shaft would be up at two in the afternoon, and the men would go for a wash in the baths at the pithead. Before this facility was provided, we had a tin bath in the house, and he used to wash in front of the coal fire.

I can only just remember the tin bath, which leaned up

against the wall of the house, and the water boiling on the fire. It seems romantic, but it was back-breaking work, especially for the women of the house, who boiled the water and carried it to the bath. This same bath would also be used to wash all our garments, and to soak the dirty working clothes over night. In our house, we were always soaking clothes, so much so that, many a time, I thought my father's trousers would become a fish.

He would call into the pit canteen for an ounce of tobacco for his pipe, light it, always with a match, and enjoy a smoke. The canteen had a back entrance near our backdoor. He would puff his pipe, smoke all around his face and over his head. He was an untidy smoker. The smoke would never go in the right direction. He did not care; he would enjoy his smoke, come snow, rain, earthquake, pestilence or my mother.

When he saw me, he would smile and pretend he did not notice. He looked clean but with traces of coal still on his face. He would say, "Hello, boy. Who are you waiting for?"

He knew I was there to meet him, but he pretended he did not know. When I answered, "You, dad," he would say,"But I am only your father. Fancy waiting for me! You should be doing something better."

He would then smile and nod his head in approval, go into his lunch box and pull out a choc ice that he bought at the same time as his tobacco, and pretend he was given it at the pit head, to eat himself, but did not fancy it just now. He would say, with a wicked look in his eyes, "It will not keep, but melt. Would you mind eating it for me?"

My reply would always be the same: "Yes, please, daddy."

The women of the Valley seemed to manage time by the shifts their husbands worked, their worry over for yet another day when the men came safely home. The pit was a dangerous place; many people did not return. They were the victims of the Black Gold, and the danger was always in the minds of the women, but never spoken about, nor was it alluded to in conversation, in case their man's turn was next.

The daily grind was hard, in a Valley where life was cheap when measured against King Coal. There seemed to be a ritualistic thanksgiving by the woman of the house, every time her man came home after his shift. It was a generally regarded superstition that it would spell bad luck if the meal were served late, something similar to crossing on the stairs, or walking under a ladder.

The woman would sit next to her husband, without speaking a word. Eyes wide open, watching with satisfaction and love, as her man, home and safe for another day, enjoyed the ritualistic offering of food. My mother was no exception to this tradition. Come what may, the meal must be on the table in front of my father before he sat down. Failure to do this was to invite bad luck over the doorstep, so the timing was measured in seconds and had a deep meaning and significance out of all proportion to its value. In today's world, with fast food and eating at all hours, it seems amusing if not laughable that these values were important, but it was the *Valley Way* of saying, "I love you," and, "I will do all I can to keep you safe."

When my father was due home after work, there would be a flurry of activity in the house. The dinner plate would be waiting to be filled with food. Many times I wondered what would happen if the plate ate the food before my father. It would have to be quick; no prisoners were taken in our house when it came to food.

After my father had finished, his plate would be that clean, you could have placed it back into the cupboard without washing it. Of course, it was always washed. This was the way the men folk said thank you and showed appreciation; there was a correlation between the clean plate and happiness: it showed that all was well.

After he had eaten, and enjoyed a smoke in the chair by the

fire, my father would be ready for the garden. He had a large vegetable plot around the corner from our house. His father gave him this plot, and he used to tell me that it had often put food on the table when times were hard.

The garden was always in pristine condition. No weeds would grow there unless they had express authority from my father to survive, and this sanction was not given. A quarter of the garden would be given over to potatoes; the rest was planted with all kinds of other vegetables. There were a few apple trees in the top of the garden, and a few rose bushes, but the garden was basically functional and used to supply our house with fresh food all the year round. Everything would be grown from seeds, often collected the year before and stored and dried in the garden shed. All the ashes from the fire went into the garden, and all organic waste from the house would find its way there and be composted.

The garden was my father's pride and joy; he had a way, like his father, of making things grow. At the top of the garden was a gate leading into a large, sloping field that formed part of the mountain. This was also my father's ground. In the past, he had kept pigs, horses, chickens and ducks in this field, but now it contained cows. It would be my job to clean out the cowshed, bring the manure in the wheelbarrow to the garden, and dig it into the ground. It was hard work, but I enjoyed it and would rather be in the garden, digging manure, than at school. The manure was stored for a year outside the cowshed; new manure needed to rot down first, to be of value. This was the real stuff, full of worms and smell, and would always produce top quality vegetables. The rest of the manure we would spread over the fields, to nourish the grass and increase its value for the cattle.

The smell of rotting manure, when it is being moved, can be described in two words: bloody awful. The whole of Cwmparc knew when this was happening, and doors would remain firmly shut against the smell. My father used to believe that, the stronger the smell, the greater the potency of the manure, therefore, the greater the vegetable crop. Smell never hurt anyone, he believed, so there can be no problem. He would puff his pipe, sparks flying everywhere as the smoke covered his face, look up and say, "The wind is bound to change direction shortly. Breathe through your mouth and you will not smell it."

He used to say that, if you couldn't breathe through your mouth, you were lacking in character. Of course, no one wished to be lacking character, and, even if they could not breathe through their mouths, they were not about to admit it. Many times, I heard the comment, the smell is hardly noticeable, which showed they must all have had strong characters. My character must have been very weak, because I could still smell the foul stench, but I did not admit it. This is how he used to get round the situation of the smell. I often heard the men telling their wives to stop moaning about the smell.

"Be of good character, and breathe through your mouth."

To this day, I do not know what smell had to do with character, or breathing through the mouth, but my father could obviously see a strong connection! The smell seemed to linger in the air for days, around the top of Cwmparc, especially on warm days, when the clouds were low in the sky. The valley would act as a trap, holding the smell in its grip like the jaws of a vice would hold a block of wood, tight and unmovable. The smell would be trapped in my clothes and hair, after I had been working in the field and garden all day. If you planted seeds in my hair, they would instantly grow in the fertilizer left on me, or curl up and die with the smell. My mother would say I was safe from the Devil, smelling like that.

"You would do the gypsies proud," she used to say.

My mother would buy into none of this character-building philosophy of breathing through the mouth. This was attributed to her being born at the bottom of Cwmparc. My father was always trying to build her character, when she disagreed with him. The thought was good, but my father never made any progress in this department, and was firmly blamed for the smell. There was no way she would be reasoned with; her mind was made up. She would look my father firmly in the eyes and say, "You can puff that pipe till the cows come home; there is nothing wrong with my character; the smell is everywhere, Dai. Sort it."

He would then look at me and say,"There are certain times in the month when women will not respond to character building," and leave it at that.

In my mother's case, I reasoned, it was every day of the month, for the full twelve months in every year, since her stance never changed. My father would say to me, with a smile,"Your mother is a gem, a no nonsense woman," carry on puffing his pipe, and go down to the pub to meet his friends, who knew all about character-building, and leave my mother to contemplate her lack of moral fibre.

I was not allowed into the house until my clothes were taken off and I had washed in the bowl my mother brought to the back door for the purpose; this also applied to my father. After washing, we would be allowed into the house, and food would be ready. These meals are as fresh today in my memory as the freshly gathered vegetables from my father's garden that made up the meal. My father believed in total freshness when it came to his food.

The plate was always full, and we would be looked over by my mother until the plate was empty. To leave even a potato would result in an interrogation about our health and wellbeing on a par with an interrogation by the Gestapo. It was easier to leave the plate clean, or feed the dog that was trained to eat vegetables, under the table, in silence.

Chapter 2

I WAS ABOUT EIGHT years old. I know this because my younger brother was not yet born, and I am eight years older than him. My other brother was two years younger than I but was too young to work in the garden. Two years is not a lot, but when you are eight, it makes you feel grown up, and your brother seems to be no more than a baby. I would not play with him because I would be doing grown up things.

Our house was at the top of the valley, in the last block of terraced houses before the mountain. We had a small front garden, which made us feel proud, because a lot of the houses opened directly onto the street. The back garden was as wide as the house, which would now seem to be very narrow and small, but, to us, it was big. It had a toilet at the bottom end. The back door, next to the toilet, led straight into the back lane. In front of our back door was another terraced block, behind which was the pit, with a winder clearly showing above the rooftops.

The winder looked like a giant giraffe, waiting to pounce and eat the slates below. The large round wheel would be continually going round in a never ending cycle that would draw the eyes upward to the top of the giant steel structure. This made you feel like an ant, trying to avoid the giant tentacles of a monster, and cables seemed to be everywhere you looked. The large, steel feet of this blight on the Valley seemed to have the sole objective of trying to squash the last ounce of profit from an already exploited people.

Next to the winder was the stack, a large, round, red brick monstrosity pointing to the sky. The top emitted a dirty, black smoke that would cling to the top of this eyesore and rain down a never-ending cycle of filth, as if to bring degradation to the occupants living below. It would take more than this to break the spirit of the people. Their strength of mind goes deep, and the will to survive is unfathomable.

The valley and its people had plenty of spirit and souls as stubborn as the coal they mined. They were more than a match for all the degradation descending upon them. It would take a lot more than dirt to blight their powerful spirits.

Looking at the two objects side-by-side, you had the feeling they were in competition with each other, vying for the prize of most obnoxious entity; the one making a continuous noise and throwing grease and coal dust from its steel ropes, the other ceaselessly blowing out smoke and making different patterns on the skyline, to attract your attention. Taking the two together, I felt they were equally successful in polluting the environment they were supposed to enhance.

Often, my mother would complain that the clothes on the line would have to be rinsed through again because, "They have been had," she would bellow, with enough force instantly to light any fire.

The neighbours reckoned she had a bell in every tooth, and a few on her fingers, since you could hear the sound of her voice above the colliery sounds. In any competition for decibels, she would have the edge over any human, animal or pit. She would rant and shout, arms flying in the air, head moving from side to side, clothes' pegs in hands, charging up and down in the back garden with the ferocity of a lioness protecting her cubs. She washed these clothes, and it seemed as if she was daring the coal dust and smoke to repose on her clean garments.

If I were a speck of dust, I would not go anywhere near my mother's clothesline. She would swear with the rage of a bull, in a totally unfeminine manner, and say, spitting and spluttering, "The pit will be the death of me."

When she was on the warpath, front doors were firmly closed

and the occupants pretended they were not at home. The only other time this happened was when the insurance man called for the weekly premium. On occasions, the neighbours were happier to see him than my mother in full flight. Her ginger hair would be in total disarray, neck red through anger, and a look on her face that would frighten the dragons out of Wales.

My father, at this stage of the show, would be totally unconcerned. We would all be running for cover and he would be running for his pipe and tobacco, light the end of the hollow where he just pressed in the tobacco, and say to my mother,"You are going to have a headache in a minute."

Her reply would be, "If I catch the owner of the pit he will need more than an aspirin for his headache, I would knock his bloody block off."

My father's reply would be, "You will go to prison."

She answered short and sharp, "I'll swing for him; I'll swing for the sod," bang the clothes with a stick, as if to beat up the dust and to warn the smoke to keep away, march indoors, and be out of sorts for the day.

My father would then give her an aspirin with a glass of water, go down the fish & chip shop and return, twenty minutes later, with a meal firmly wrapped in newspaper. My mother would instantly respond to the smell of the food, and the aspirin would have the desired effect, when taken in conjunction with the fish and chips. My mother would moan that the last thing she needed was food, even as she was eating the chips, two at a time, and pulling the fish apart with the finesse of a wart hog.

My mother maintained that fish and chips must be eaten out of the paper, or the true flavour would be lost. She would attack the paper with the same ferocity as the dust on the clothes-line; place the empty paper in the fire to burn, and then tell my father that she was not really hungry, and to ask next time, before he goes to the fish shop. My father would nod his head, say sorry, and do exactly the same thing again.

My father was placid with a slight trait of stubbornness; my mother was stubborn with not the slightest trait of placidity at any time. Even when she was trying to be quiet and reserved, the result would normally be her explaining where we went wrong in annoying her, and giving us advice on how to be good citizens. She wanted the world to know she was no pushover, and made a big show of being in control, even if she was totally out of her depth. She had an answer for most things and, where there was no answer, she would invent one to suit the current situation.

To reinforce this tendency, she would always say to my father, "I won't ask you for advice because I know you will agree, isn't that so, Dai?"

My father would nod his head during the conversation, to show approval of the situation. He developed this approval technique into a fine art, nodding and murmuring at precisely the right second, in tune with my mother's full stops. Fortunately, they were few and far between because to get a word in edgeways was quite a feat, when my mother had something to say, which was all the time, except when she was asleep, and even then, I had my doubts. My father used to say my mother had a plaster for every sore, and if there were no sore, she would still stick a plaster on, so that it fitted in with her explanation of the circumstances.

She had a heart of gold, provided she was approached in the right way.

Her heart was, "true gold," my father remarked. "She has true grit and a rage that would temper stone." He used to say this with a smile on his face and a look of contentment in his eyes. This anger was never directed at the family, but to anyone else, animal, mineral or even smoke, that tried to put us down or to take an unfair advantage of her family or friends. If there were a battle to be fought or a problem that needed sorting the neighbours would enlist my mother to the battlefield, to help and coordinate the action.

"Get Lol," would be the battle cry. "She will know what to do."

She was a formidable opponent; a typical valley person, who went to London during the war, to work as a home help, and this, she thought, gave her the edge in the ways of the world. My father liked the quiet life and was happiest when in his garden, and able to have his pint of beer and his ounce of pipe tobacco, his little luxuries, as he called them.

One occasion, we were both in the garden together, sitting at the top of the vegetable plot, on a bench my father had made. He had his pipe in his mouth; I was watching ladybirds moving up and down the plants, after aphids.

He said, "Move closer by my side, boy; there is something you should know about life when you get older. If you are able to hold this thought in your mind you will always be happy".

I knew he had something important to tell me.

"The world is a big place. I have not travelled as much as your mother, or lived away from home; my education in the conventional sense is poor, and I am not even well read. When it comes to life and how to conduct your life on this earth, I *am well read* and schooled in what is right and wrong."

I looked at him and was just about to speak when he started again.

"Some people say there is no right or wrong. Do not listen, do not take that first step, do not be taken in. Listen to your inner self and, if things are wrong, do not follow that path. There is a right and a wrong way, and it is often easier and more profitable to follow the wrong way in the short term; *but wrong will be out in the end,* and it will be too late if this is the pathway you have followed.

"Repentance is no more than trying to undo the knot you have tied in the past and asking for another chance; keep the rope straight at all times. Do not tie yourself up in knots."

I did not see how a knot was wrong, and it would be years later before this message hit home, long after my father had died.

My response to this was as a child would answer.

"It can't be wrong to kill a fly, daddy. That is not wrong."

My father reflected for a minute and answered, "What if you were the fly," and he let the subject drop. These words have cascaded down the years with me and have been kept firmly locked into the clay of my heart, slowly forming into a river that I have tried to follow in my journey through life.

My father was, indeed, an educated man. He would smile, puff his pipe, look around the garden, ruffle my hair with his hands and say, "When you are older, you will understand and hold these memories, long after I am gone."

How so right he was when he spoke these words of wisdom.

Chapter 3

ALL HIS FREE TIME was spent in the garden, my father's haven from the hardness of the valley. On one side of the garden was an evergreen hedge, always cut and in shape. A distant family relative planted the hedge and, years ago it became my grandfather's duty to be its guardian. By constant grooming, it had become an object of beauty. The hedge was full size before my father was born, and he used to tell me that these trees are family friends. They knitted together in a friendly and welcoming way, as if each tree belonged exactly where it was growing; each branch moulded by the constant cutting and shaping by generations of my family on my father's side, until it formed a green wall. It was so dense that you would have great difficulty in placing your hand inside it.

The hedge was ideal for birds to nest inside, safe in the knowledge that cats cannot get to them. The hedgerows were a haven for wild life, not just for the birds but also for hedgehogs, mice, voles, and all the other wild creatures you would expect to find in a garden but you rarely see. My father knew where they were hiding and how to see them. Many times he would stop and ask me to look carefully into the leaves, pointing to the ground and asking me what I could see. I could see only the garden leaves and the earth, but my father would see and recognize the creatures of the garden, hidden just below the surface but to be seen if you knew where to look.

My father knew where every nest was situated and how long the construction had taken.

"There is new life in the garden today. Look in the hedge," he would say, pointing to the exact spot, and he would be right.

He would know when the nests were being built, the day the eggs were laid, and how long before the eggs would hatch. My father valued all creatures. They all deserved a chance to make the most of life, he would say. He placed great store on giving everyone a fair chance.

The hedge was his pride and joy. He looked after the trees as if they were made of precious metal.

"They are family friends, and friendship is given from the heart, and should not be measured against material things; always remember that," he once stated.

His father had handed down the trees, and he was now their guardian. He used to say to me, "Accumulate what you will, but no matter what you think you own, it is but a loan, and you must give it back at your journey's end."

Many different types of birds visited and made their home in our garden, and were all made welcome by my father.

"They have a right to be here," he would say. "We must all recognize that we share the same space, and it is our duty to make it comfortable for each other."

There was one particular bird that stood out, as far as my father was concerned: the song thrush. He would spend hours watching these birds.

We would sit still at the top of the garden, seeing the birds looking for the food my father placed around the garden. It was my father's way of sharing. The birds would be everywhere, sparrows, robins, blackbirds, starlings, and song thrushes, coming in and out of the garden all day long.

The birds had no fear of my father. It was as if they knew he was their friend, and often they would come so close you could touch them. I was told never to try and catch them.

"They are untamed creatures, and they fear captivity. Friendship is about freedom, not restriction. Allow the birds to make their own choice. You must not entice them in with food and then entrap them. That is betrayal, not friendship."

He would forcefully tell me, measuring every word with great exactness, to make doubly sure I got and understood the message.

The reason my father preferred the song thrush, goes back to his youth, when he reared five of them from chicks, and this fondness for the thrush stayed with him all his life. Even at a young age, he knew where all the nests were in the hedge, and one day, he noticed that a nest with five chicks inside was not being looked after and the chicks were unfed. A kestrel or a cat could have caught them, but without intervention the lot would die. The centre of the hedge was dense and there was safety inside, and as long as they were fed, there was a chance they would survive.

The way my father achieved this still fascinates me today. He obtained a bundle of bulrushes from the mountain and tied them together in the form of a loose rope. A mixture of bread and milk was prepared and mashed down into a sticky pulp. One end of the bulrushes was then dipped into the prepared food. The end with the food was placed into the hedge, just above the nest. By moving the rushes slowly back and fore the little creatures were encouraged to eat. My father would do this task several times every day, supplementing the diet with small worms and snails, as the chicks got older. They were able to feed from the food stuck to the end of the rushes, without being frightened and with the minimum of disruption to the hedge and nest.

When speaking to me about these little creatures, I could feel the warmth and kindness emanating from his body. He felt proud of the way he helped these birds on their way. He once told me,

"We pass this way but once. If there is any kindness you can do, do it now, boy, for tomorrow might be too late."

I have thought of these words many times and he is, of course right. If he had left the chicks until later, they would all have died. Not one of the little birds was lost. About a week before they were to venture from the nest, my father became quite agitated about the situation. He felt that, without the adult birds to guide them they would fall easy prey to cats and the rats in the garden. So he decided to catch all the chicks and continue to rear them from the safety of the garden shed. He knew that they must all be caught together. If they were alarmed and went from the nest startled it would be almost impossible to catch them, and their chances of survival would be gone. He began by feeding them until they were really full. It was almost dark before this task was completed, and the evening, after feeding, was the best time to catch and move them to the shed.

A few days before this, he built a temporary haven for the birds. He obtained a tea chest, and punctured holes all around the sides to allow light into the interior. He then built a platform made of clay at the centre of the chest, incorporating the same materials into the clay as the nest. Branches were collected from the hedge and placed all round the centre, to create the same environment as the hedge. The holes in the box acted like the hedge, throwing light into the centre of the box, penetrating to the middle, recreating the same light effect as the hedge would: a dappled type of diffused light.

The branches were held in place by wet clay, moulded into each branch to create the illusion of a tight knit hedge. The clay, when dried, would hold the branches tight in place, keeping them from moving. Leaves were placed at the bottom of the chest, to reconstruct the hedge floor. The chest was placed near the light, directly in the window, and turned every few hours, to create a different light effect inside the box.

The way he moved the birds is also worth mentioning; it really shows how his mind worked and the values he held as a young boy. He traced each branch around the base of the nest and nicked them with his knife. He cut these branches through, one by one, leaving only a few to cut to move the nest. He then cut these last few branches, and the nest was now clear to be moved. This was all done slowly, so as not to alarm the chicks. He was now able to remove the whole nest together with the branches to the new location in the chest.

Before this, the birds needed to be secured, or they would panic and leave the nest. Bulrushes were placed all around the nest in a circle, dipped beforehand in the bread and milk mulch. The birds were used to seeing the rushes and associated them with food, so there would be no problem in placing these rushes around the nest without alarming the occupants. When this was completed, wet clay was worked into the rushes from the outside, to give them structure and an element of strength for the move.

The top of the nest, with the rushes around it, was covered with see-through gauze. The whole structure could now be easily moved to the shed. My father reasoned that the tree would not miss a few branches and would soon grow back to its former density. The nest was placed in the centre of the box and secured with the clay to the rest of the other branches.

The birds were successfully moved and the interior of the chest looked like the inside of the hedge. The amount of work that must have gone into this transformation would have taken days. I was told that he worked right through the night on one occasion, to get the box ready. When my father had a task to complete, he would focus on it totally until it was completed.

He continued feeding the chicks until they were ready to be released into the garden. He trained the birds to fend for themselves, by ceasing to feed them two weeks before they were due to be released. Snails and worms were left in the box, for them to find for themselves. The box was moved into the garden and placed on top of four posts knocked into the ground. The side of the box was opened, exposing the birds to the wild outdoors. They stayed in the nest for a while, and then they were gone.

I asked my father why he did not keep the birds. They belonged to him; after all, he had saved their life. Why spend all this time looking after them, only to let them go? They would be always safe and well fed, they could have the full run of the shed, and they would still belong to my father and every one would be happy.

He said, "You have overlooked one main point: they never belonged to me in the first place. They belong to the land and the countryside. I was only helping them on their way. It was their time to move on, just as your time will come to fly the nest and make your way in the world. To deny any one this right is to deny them their freedom."

"Did you ever see the birds again?" I asked. He was quite shocked at this statement.

"This is their garden; they were born here. This garden belongs to them; they are a part of the garden as much as that tree," he said, pointing to one of the trees in the garden.

"If they are still in the garden and you see them every day," I said innocently, "they are not free, otherwise they would be gone."

He lit his pipe, thought for a minute and answered, "Freedom is about the ability to choose where you wish to be, to spend time, to suit yourself. To be free, you must be there by your own free will."

I replied, "By letting the birds go free, you gave them different options, and they chose to stay, so the act of giving them freedom resulted in them staying. They were captives in their own garden, since that is where they wished to be."

My father smiled at this comment and looked round the garden in satisfaction. "You got it," he said. "If you wish to keep something close to you, give it the ability to fly away but make the staying a lot better."

I can understand his words more clearly now. He meant them in the context of the garden, but these thoughts could be applied to life generally. If this philosophy were followed today, the world would be a better place, and true freedom would be within everyone's grasp.

Chapter 4

MY MOTHER ALWAYS looked big to me, and so when she became pregnant, I did not notice the difference. She never seemed to change. She was a big, powerful woman, dressed in a working overall with a small shawl-type cardigan over her shoulders. The overall had large pockets and there were always a few clothes pegs in them; the skirt came below the knee, and she wore flat, functional, hardwearing shoes. She looked as if she was always ready for work, on everlasting guard in case the dust and grime of the pit tried to sneak past her into our house. She used to stand at the front door, sweeping brush in hand, hoping to frighten the dirt away before it had a chance to enter.

Looking at her in this stance, I could understand where the battle cry, "Get Lol," originated. Change her clothes for armour, and her brush for a lance, and there you have it: a woman ready for battle and prepared to protect her family at all costs. She seemed to me to be always on standby, but she never progressed past this point. It was as if she were always waiting for something to happen. She would sweep the front of the house with triumphant force; brush down tight to the floor, in a rugby scrum with the flagstones, as if she was fighting for Wales. The flat flagstones did not stand a chance; the grime and dirt would be flying in all directions, with my mother head down low to the floor, false teeth firmly closed.

On this particular day, walking home from school, I was stopped by Uncle Mog, and he said, "Your mother is not very well just now."

He told me that I was to have tea with him. My uncle lived

on the opposite side of the road, about six doors down from our house, and I used to spend a lot of time with him, walking on the mountain tops that were still left green, and not corrupted by the black dust.

I spent most of the evening in my uncle's house, and, at about eight o'clock, my father came over to see me and said, "I have a surprise for you."

He was wearing a broad smile. I thought for a moment and knew it could not be a surprise choc ice because he was not coming home from work. Perhaps it was extra pocket money.

"I like surprises. Tell me, tell me quickly," I answered impatiently.

My father never was one for long explanations and it came straight out.

"There is an addition to the family; you have a baby brother."

"What do you mean? I never said I wanted another brother," I replied, rather taken back. The first thing I thought about was, brother or no brother, I am not sharing my bed or any of my choc ices with any one.

I had not the slightest idea my mother was having a baby. I did not know what to expect. My father was happy and smiling, and he placed his hand on my shoulder, looked straight into my eyes and said, bursting with delight, "This is a good day. There is new life in the house today."

"Does it talk?" I enquired.

"Not just yet, but it will when older," he replied.

This must be good, I reasoned, remembering the garden and how my father used to tell me to look in the hedge and leaves. When this happened, we were happy and excited, so new life in the house must be good. I had visions of my father looking into the hedge or under the leaves in the garden, to show me the new arrival. How my mother would get under the hedge to have the baby I did not know. I supposed that the baby would have to be born quickly, because my mother could not keep still for more than a few minutes.

My Father sat me down, and gave me time to relax, lit his pipe. Then, he knelt down by my side, his head at the same level as mine, and said,"Remember the five little song thrushes in the garden? Which one did I love the best?"

This seemed a strange question. He had just said I had another brother, and now he was talking about the birds in the garden. I thought for a while, my father looked at me, pipe in mouth, smoke all around his face, sparks shooting out of the end of his pipe. He was waiting for me to reply. He was the most patient person I have ever had the privilege to know.

I did not have an answer. He never told me he loved any one of the birds more than the rest. He loved them all equally, each as important as the next.

I replied, "You did not tell me you loved any one of the birds more than the others. They were all loved equally." I did not understand the point he was trying to make. To me, all the birds were the same, "What if there were six birds; would the last one be of any less value than the fifth?"

"It would still be loved in exactly the same way, even if there were twenty." I replied, thinking I was being clever with this last remark, but my father was ahead of me.

"Your new brother is like an extra bird, a welcome addition to our family, and will be loved in the same way as I love you and your other brother. The family will change, but for the better."

He held me in his arms for a few seconds and we went out of the house and across the road, hand-in-hand, to see my new brother.

My mother was in bed, upstairs in the front bedroom. She looked red in the face, and her hair was wet and stuck to the side of her cheek. I could only see her head; the rest of her body was tucked up under the bedclothes. I remember how clean and tidy the bedroom looked, furniture all in place, the bed taking up most of the small room, with a closed bible by the side of the bed, but I had the feeling it had recently been read.

The curtains were closed against the night, but there was enough light in that small bedroom to eclipse the sun. You could feel and touch the warmth in the air. The very walls of the room seemed to move and shimmer, bouncing back happiness at you with the speed of atoms moving through space, as if dancing in the joy of the moment.

My other brother, who was being looked after by a neighbour, came into the bedroom a little later, and his first questions were, "Where is my tea? Why is it late? I am hungry?"

Our mother spoke to both of us and said, "My boys, you both have a new brother."

Her voice was faint and there were tears in her eyes as she looked at us and at the new baby. This behaviour was new to me; she looked so weak and tired, not what you would expect from my mother.

From under the bedclothes, wrapped in a blanket, she drew a little bundle, and at the end of this blanket was a little face, small and red, eyes closed. We both sat on the bed and, in turn, my brother and I held the little bundle in our arms. My father took an active role in this task, making sure we held the baby tight into our laps, protecting the head of the baby with his hand.

So, the third brother had arrived; we were now five. I remember thinking how small the baby looked and being thankful there were no namby pamby girls in our family, not thinking for one minute that my mother was one. To me, she was just my mother, not a woman or a girl, but a solid rock that would forever look after us. She would always be there; to live without her was not something I could even contemplate.

My experience of death was in the context of the garden; it was here where my father explained the way life moves on. It seemed natural, the way my father explained it to me, the moving on. For the first time, it dawned on me that I am part of this moving on, in the same way as things in the garden move on. There was no difference. We are born and we must also move on, when our time comes. It was a shock, realising nothing ever stays the same, and the only constant in life is change.

To see my mother weak and in bed after the birth made me think for the first time how fragile life really is, and how the fate of the family can easily change. She looked at us with her deep brown eyes and, in a quiet voice devoid of strength, said, "You boys are my whole life and I love you all." She then turned her head slowly and looked to my father, as if to say, "Didn't I do well?"

My father nodded as if to say, "Yes, you did very well." It was as if there was a secret language between the two, to which only they held the code. If my mother made a statement, my father would automatically agree. He would nod his head, smile, look my mother firmly in the eyes, and keep his mouth firmly closed.

The new arrival changed things more than I had anticipated. The baby needed feeding on a regular basis. This meant we often had to wait for our food until the baby was fed and changed. Napkins were purchased from the pit canteen; they were cheaper there than in the shops, as were the towels. My father used to bring a few home every week, and the older nappies would be reconstituted as dish cloths. Nothing was ever wasted.

The bath was in use day and night. My father's working clothes were now relegated to the back yard and left until the napkins were clean. There were baby clothes everywhere; the house was full with the signs and smells of the new baby. The only place free from the ever present mark of the baby was in the outdoor toilet. To this haven of contemplation at the bottom of the garden I would retreat when the baby was crying, safe in the knowledge that, if my mother shouted, I could pretend I could not hear her. This was difficult, for when she started calling, you could hear her in the next street.

The baby was always transported in a shawl; this is a wonderful Welsh invention that you seldom see nowadays. It consisted of a blanket, wrapped around the waist of the woman, over the shoulders, around the back and tucked in under the arms, to form a complete circle. The baby is deposited in the front of the shawl and is held firmly in the wrap, freeing woman's hands for other tasks.

I would see my mother walking up and down the house and garden, with the baby wrapped in the shawl, tapping its back and giving comfort. My father also took his turn in this, and would wrap the shawl around himself and walk up and down the garden, trying to get the baby to sleep. These are my early remembrances of life in our house, controlled by the actions of the colliery, which seemed to pierce every part of our existence, as we went about our life at the top of the Valley in Cwmparc.

Chapter 5

A T THIS EARLY AGE I developed a love of the mountains, and was allowed to walk them with my uncle Mog, a rather short individual with a pleasant rounded face and short stumpy legs, arms like a pit pony, a stout neck and a sharp wit.

"There is open space and freedom on the mountains," he once confided in me. He was a true mountain walker and knew every inch of the mountain within twenty miles of Cwmparc. He had a reputation as a hard worker and he prized himself on his building expertise. He would always complete the job, no matter how difficult. He had one main philosophy: if it did not fit, or if there were difficulty in the completion, or he felt the work was moving too slowly, he would knock it into place with his hammer. One way or another, things would eventually fit.

"The hammer is a marvellous tool," he would inform me, when instructing me in home improvements.

He was always available to help the neighbours tile roofs, hang doors, fix drainpipes, and repair fences; he would also help my father and mother and his brothers, whether they needed help or not. He could be described as a compulsive helper. It was his addiction. I am sure, on many occasions, when, to satisfy this compulsion by helping in the garden and house, he went down Chepstow Road to see his parents and his married brother Davy, who also lived there with his wife, it would fall on my uncle Davy to try and control this fever.

"Keep him talking and ply him with food before the compulsion gets a firm hold," he would quietly whisper to Peg, his wife.

There was many a time when Davy would have to go over a job after Mog, but he was unable to hurt his brother's feelings, and tell him.

"You could always tell Mog's trademark," his brother Davy would say. "Look for the hammer marks on the job, and the cement on the floor, and you know Mog had a hand in the construction."

Often I would find him busy at a task, swearing at a door or wall as if the objects were human and they could understand his anger and frustration.

"You have been warned," he would bellow at a wall he just plastered, as some of the render worked loose. "This is the last bloody chance you are having to stay on the wall." He would shout loudly, as if the job could understand. "Now, stop being difficult and stay on the wall, or I will resort to heavier treatment," pointing his trowel at the offending plaster as if threatening to stab it with the point.

A cigarette would always be sticking out of his mouth, held firmly between his gums, his two black teeth clearly showing between his lips, a flat cap on his bald head, and clothes hanging loosely over his body, he looked every inch the tradesman. He also worked in the pit, and would say proudly, "You are looking at a man that has never lost a shift through drink," to anyone who would listen, even though he enjoyed his few pints of beer, and sometimes more than a few.

The only grandparents I remember were those on my mother's side, living in Chepstow Road. This street was half way down Cwmparc, off the main road, and built on the side of a hill. The walk to my grandparents' house would take about thirty minutes. The trek to Chepstow with my uncle Mog, a few times every month, was an event I looked forward to. We would always travel the back way; this meant the lane way at the back of the terraced houses. Mog would say, "We will travel the Gully Way."

We always travelled the same way, except on New Year's Day, and then we travelled the main road and turned up by the Cooperative into the bottom end of Chepstow, and continued straight up the hill.

We would always start from the back door of my uncle's house, follow the back lanes until we reached the lane in Chepstow, thirty minutes later; talking to everyone we met on the way down, including the dogs. We would always walk side by side. Mog would have a walking stick in one hand, and be chewing gum as well as having the cigarette in his mouth, ash always hanging from the end.

He was a popular character and would talk to anyone that would listen; even if you did not listen, he would still talk to you, walking by your side if you were in a hurry. He would have his say. There were a lot of my mother's qualities in him. It was better to resign yourself to a few minutes chat at the offset, than to resist; there was no escape from him. In truth, because he was such a character and well known, everyone used to enjoy talking to him. He was witty, courteous and well respected, as well as being always full of life. He was full of the joys of spring, no matter what the season, he was my hero, and I was proud to walk with him and call him uncle.

I was convinced that if we travelled the front way, we would never get to our destination, especially if we had to pass by the Tremains and the Park Hotel Public Houses. Even if we managed not to get caught in these havens of the valley, we still had the Dare Hotel and the Legion waiting to entrap us and hold us to ransom for a few hours. To pass these other two watering holes would be too much for any human to endure, so, to keep out of temptation, the back way it would always be, when travelling to Chepstow.

We would enter onto my grandparents' property by the door from the lane. From the door there were steps and a path leading downward to the house. The garden was extremely steep, with the back gate at the same level as the roof. As you approached the back entrance to the house, the steps were at their steepest. Steep back gardens were common in the valley; the whole place was built on the side of the mountain, without a lot of thought for the miners who would occupy them. Some of the back gardens were so steep; they could be used as training grounds for mountain goats. But we managed and indeed did not even notice; the valley was our home; the garden belonged to us, no matter how steep. It was a place where the older miners could forget the pit for a while, and spend a few hours manually working their bit of land.

This steepness did not stop after you entered the house; the inside was flat until the front door, where the steps started again, and led down to the road below. The inside was larger than our two-bedroom house but not by a great deal. All the houses were of a similar design, with two to three bedrooms, according to the layout of the street. The size of the houses did not really matter; they were our homes, and that was the only thing that mattered.

"The house is the heart of the family," my grandmother once told me, when making a cup of tea, bending over the open fire, kettle and teapot in hand. "It is the place you come home to in your time of trouble."

These words are familiar in all languages and cultures and are as relevant today as they were then.

The first recollection I have of my grandfather is of him sitting in his garden, behind the lane we used to travel to arrive at his house. You would come out of his back door, cross the lane and go straight into the garden. There were lots of plots all around, where some people kept pigs, a few looked after dogs, others had ducks and pigeons, but there would always be a vegetable plot.

My grandfather spent all his free time in the garden, tending his pigs and chickens and a menagerie of other animals. He also kept a vegetable plot, but for the last few years he had needed help from his sons to keep his garden in order. He would be dressed in old clothes; a flat cap on his head, and he would be known affectionately as the old man to his sons, and pop to his grandchildren. My grandmother would be called mam mam.

He used to let me play in the garden, and I often watched him moving about slowly, coughing continually and uncontrollably, because of the dust from the Black Gold in his lungs. He would often say, "I am shot through with dust."

The coal was taking its revenge on my grandfather, as it extracted revenge on all the people in the Valley that went into the ground to disturb its resting place of thousands of years.

He would place a rag over his mouth, cough into it, and show me the dark, creeping, foul, black dust that was draining the life out of him. This was inside his body, strangling his lungs with the force of an anaconda, and would kill him before his time.

If only these romantics could see how my grandfather was suffering every minute of every day, unable to walk more than a few steps, before stopping and rasping and gasping for breath, they would realise the hardships and sacrifices these people were making in the name of progress. They paid a high price to feed their families and to help the British Economy.

Like all other members of my family, my grandfather enjoyed his pint of beer, and attended the Park Legion regularly, to keep up this long-standing tradition. This is where the men gathered to talk about men things, or so they would have you believe. I could never quite work out what they would have to talk about this early in the evening and every weekend, but whatever it was, it must have been important. To be late for these essential meetings would be to let the side down. The conversation would start as soon as the doors opened.

To be sure to be on time, everyone would arrive half an hour beforehand, in case the Legion doors opened early, and the discussion started without them. When I got a bit older, I understood that they were there for one reason only, the beer, and would arrive early in order not to miss any time at the bar. The women were ahead of the game and encouraged their husbands out early, for a bit of peace and quiet.

It would take my grandfather half an hour to walk to the Legion that was no more than a few minutes from his house. He would start early. He could only take a few steps at a time and needed to stop to get his breath. Many times I saw him holding on to the wall, panting for breath before moving a few more steps on his way to or from his house. This was not just my grandfather's illness; it was common throughout the whole valley.

If you worked in the pit you expected to have dust in your lungs. It was a common sight to see older miners walking a few steps and stopping to rest, cough, spit, and move on a few steps further. These sights will remain in my mind for the rest of my life. These men, destroyed by the Black Gold, were a privilege to know; they were a breed unto themselves, as well as being part of my family.

The respect I hold for them, including my grandfather, is as high as the stars; indeed, they were stars to me and will always shine brightly in my mind. They had to go into the earth to work for a living, but they will always be the salt of the earth, true, solid people, crippled and exhausted through years of exploitation, but still full of Valley Pride.

As the months progressed, my grandfather got worse; we were all concerned. The doctor was now a frequent visitor to Chepstow Road. The coughing seemed to be deeper and more prolonged, and the old man could now only manage a step, or at the most two, before stopping to obtain breath. He was continually in combat, struggling to move forward, but in reality, he was losing ground daily, with every passing breath. To watch this brave man, even braver than the soldier trying to hold his ground against insurmountable odds, it made me cry many times, when in the toilet alone, with only my thoughts for company. I was old enough to know what death was and its finality. The anaconda would be eating soon, and its grip was tightening on my grandfather. His face continually struggled to keep its shape as his body fought for the air we all take for granted.

Within a matter of a few weeks, pop was confined to bed; his weight loss now apparent, the strong muscles that once could shift a ton of coal in a blink of an eye had already lifted the last lump. I remember visiting him in bed, his eyes sunken and glazed, but he was conscious and still able to understand and talk, in between the coughing and the constant rasping for breath, but he was in continuous pain.

The suffering was intense and I wished it would stop and go away. Hating the way I was thinking, I knew that the stopping would result in only one outcome. A member of the family would sit in the bedroom every night. He would not be alone at the end. This would be a betrayal of their father, when he breathed his last breath.

I felt ashamed of my thoughts, part of me wishing he would fight the Black Gold in his lungs, but the rest of me feeling he had suffered enough and hoping that death would be swift. This smell of death in that small room was well masked with disinfectant, and clean sheets, changed several times every day, but this was only a mask, and, like all masks, it would eventually fall away and show death in all its nakedness.

The smell was constantly in the air that my grandfather could no longer breathe. The end was near. Incontinent and broken, he awaited his fate; ashamed that he could no longer manage the everyday tasks we perform without thought. The lesson about moving on that I was taught in the garden by my father did not seem relevant now; there was no beauty in this. I had come face-to-face with what moving on really meant. I grew up a lot that day.

The following day, my grandfather died. There were no

phones to pass on the message; the knock came at our door early in the morning. My mother, always strong, could no longer hold the line. It was expected and inevitable, but when we know a thing we dread is about to happen, we go into denial even when we know there is no hope. All expectation was now gone, there was nothing to hold on to; the full reality was felt with the force of a knife thrust between my mother's ribs. Her father was dead.

She fell into my father's arms, trying not to cry, but the composure was gone, the full force of losing her father was upon her. I felt sad but glad that the suffering was over. This was my first encounter with death and the loss of a loved one.

Our house was full of sorrow that day, my mother silent and heartbroken, sat, wordlessly, in the corner. My father said nothing but, feeling the pain with her, was powerless to stop the grief taking its course. The general consensus was that his death was a blessing in disguise, he had suffered enough.

Years later, I was reading a poem about Death by John Donne, and it reminded me of the death of my grandfather. Perhaps it was because it was a first encounter that this poem stays clearly in my mind.

Death be not proud, though some have called thee
Mighty and dreadful, for thou art not soe,
For, those, whom thou think'st, thou dost overthrow,
Die not, poore death, nor yet canst thou kill mee.
From rest and sleepe, which but thy pictures bee,
Much pleasure, then from thee, much more must flow,
And soonest our best men with thee doe goe,
Rest of their bones, and soules deliverie.
Thou art slave to fate, chance, kings, and desperate men,
And dost with poyson, warre, and sicknesse dwell,
And poppie, or charmes can make us sleepe as well,
And better then thy stroake; why swell'st thou then?
One short sleepe past, wee wake eternally,
And death shall be no more; death thou shalt die.

All focus was now on the funeral and the welfare of my granny. The undertaker was called for and my grandfather was washed and cleaned up, before being dressed in his best suit and placed into the coffin, to lie in state in the front room. I did not see him but everyone said he looked peaceful and contented away from the pain of this world. The pit could do no more harm to him.

The day of the funeral arrived, and everyone dressed in their best clothes for the event. Sandwiches were cut by the neighbours, pickles placed on trays, together with ham and cheese; beer purchased and placed in readiness. He was to have a good send off.

At first, I thought of going to the funeral. My father talked to me about what would happen and left the decision to me. I did not see even the coffin because my mother wished me to remember him alive. I decided not to go and stayed at home, the next door neighbour looking after me. I was to call if I needed anything.

As the hour for the burial approached, I went to my bedroom. I was crying, tears cascading down both cheeks, as I lay across the bed. I did not like this moving on; it was too painful.

The thought of my grandfather was in my mind, not dead, but alive in the garden, talking to me, holding out his hand to support me as we went into the pig shed. I knew he was dead, but I could see him alive, coughing and smiling. I cried alone and prayed that God would be kind to my grandfather.

There was a tradition in the Valley for the vicar to come to the house to conduct the funeral service, and, after a number of kind words about the deceased and a few prayers, the men only to go to the cemetery. The women would stay in the house, to prepare the food that would have been organised beforehand and would be eaten when the men arrive back from the cemetery.

There was another tradition: after the men returned from the burial and a decent amount of time had been spent eating the sandwiches and talking to my grandmother, the men would leave the women to wash up, and they would make their way to the Legion, to drink to the life of my grandfather. This tradition was not taken lightly. He would have a good send off, rounds of beer in vast quantities would need to be consumed, and it was a matter of principle to drink until you drop.

If you were still standing straight and upright at the end of the day, and able to speak without a slur in your voice, you were not showing the required amount of respect, and it would be time to resort to stronger tactics.

"Shall I prepare and sort out the boys from the men?" the bar tender would ask. "Yes," Mog would shout. "We are all on the double whiskies and the large brandies from now on." The send-off must be of the required standard, and the quantity of alcohol drunk would demonstrate the depth of feeling held for the departed.

My grandfather must have been extremely well liked because, by the evening, not a man could stand up straight or speak more than a few words before resorting to child speak. To substantiate this, on the following day, a headache was had by all concerned, confirming that the send off was up to standard, and so my grandfather was laid to rest.

Chapter 6

LIFE GOES ON, the past is soon relegated to memory, and my life soon returned to normal but, a few weeks later, my father started to feel ill and developed a constant pain in his legs and feet. He paid no attention to this at first, but as the pain got worse, my mother started to show concern.

"You should slow down, Dai, your legs need looking at by the doctor," she urged. "Call down tomorrow and I'll come with you."

"Don't fuss, it is nothing. I'll call down next week if they are still the same."

His legs and feet were now continually swollen and looked black. The doctor's surgery was a place other people went to wait in, to see the physician, but not my father. He would always go tomorrow, but tomorrow never came.

"You must get your legs looked at. This nonsense has gone on too long. Go tomorrow."

"Yes, yes, tomorrow," he replied.

My mother would get angry with him, stamp her feet and shout.

"You are a stubborn old sod, Dai, and I'll have none of it; do you hear me?" She was worried, and he would not listen.

"Everything is all right. Stop fussing." he answered lighting his pipe, and taking not the slightest notice. This infuriated my mother further. He was totally unfit for work but would not give in to his situation.

The doctor was called to the house. My father had no control over the situation; it had gone too far for any more pro-crastination. He was ill and my mother was determined that the doctor must see him. One look at his legs, and the doctor signed him straight into the hospital for tests. I could see the look in my mother's eyes, underplaying the situation in front of my father, face smiling and laughing, and she stating she wished she could go to the hospital instead, for a rest. The look turned into fright as she turned round; she knew the situation was serious; how serious she did not yet know, but I could see she was expecting the worst.

The ambulance was at the house in less than an hour, and my father was wrapped in a blanket and placed into a wheelchair. The doctor forbade him to place any weight on his feet.

"Your legs are in a bad way, Dai. Place as little weight on them as possible," the doctor warned. The ambulance man wheeled my father to the front door and was just trying to manoeuvre the wheelchair around the corner of the small passage, when my father said, "Stop," in a clear, no-nonsense tone, placed his hands on the wheelchair, stood up and walked to the ambulance. He looked proud, his head held high; he knew he would be battling for his life but no one, no one, would carry him out of his house, unless he were in a coffin.

The diagnosis turned out to be what was known as beat knees: the miner's cancer. The knees and feet become poisoned due to the constant pressure placed on the knee. The veins in the leg become varicose; poison builds up in the knees and feet and spreads to the rest of the body, if not treated and removed.

This toxicity will eventually become unstoppable and destroy the rest of the body. The case with my father was particularly bad; the poison was in both legs and feet; possibly also in the rest of the body, and so an operation must be undertaken immediately, to determine the extent of the problem. The years spent underground, walking and working on his knees, were now taking their toll.

Another victim on the altar of King Coal, it was now his turn to reap the reward for all his years of hard work in the black hole.

Pentwyn Hospital, at the bottom end of Cwmparc, where the operation was to take place, is about a mile from our house. My mother would walk this distance every day to see my father; often carrying the baby in her shawl. The preparation for the operation was completed in a few days, and he was ready for surgery.

I was young, but I knew we were in difficult waters and a storm was just around the corner. The full burden was firmly on my mother's shoulders; the family boat was leaking and all hands were on deck, fighting for and with my father. All my family was as one, the true *valley spirit* showing through. In the forefront of this battle and a tremendous comfort to us was my dependable uncle Mog. Over this period, he was continually back and fore to our house. Just to have him there seemed to give my mother strength, although she would never admit to this and often called him a bloody nuisance and told him to stop fussing, but I knew the truth and so did my uncle.

The first time the reality of the situation hit home to me was when a vicar from the local church visited my mother. She was sitting in the corner, bible in hand. When she saw me, her composure instantly returned but I knew. I knew because I had tasted the sting of death with my grandfather. I did not wish to be stung again. We were in a serious state of affairs.

We all visited my father at the hospital on the night before the operation. I think he had a number of visitors that day, but I am unable to remember who they all were. My mother, to the outside world, was a tower of strength. The neighbours used to wonder how she could cope and show no sign of weakness. I used to think this myself. The only person who really knew the truth was Mog. He was like a steadfast rock for my mother. All the other family members rallied round but I hope they will understand the special feeling we all had for Mog.

We were the last to visit, my mother, my two younger brothers and me, with steadfast Mog in the background, trying to keep out of the way but not doing a very good job. Pigs would fly, and we would be shooting for bacon, before Mog could be kept in the background for long.

A few minutes before they called time on visiting, he touched my father's hand and his head as only a friend could, looked him in the eyes, held the glance for a few seconds and said,

"Good luck, Dai. You know your kids will want for nothing. See you tomorrow. I will be outside, having a cigarette."

He walked away, leaving us to spend the last few minutes together. I remember looking at my father, kissing him and saying, "See you tomorrow, daddy."

Mog came back, wordlessly took the baby from my mother, steered me and my brother to the door, and said,

"I have a few sweets in my pocket."

It was years later before I realised the tact and thoughtfulness behind this small act.

After my mother left the ward, the preparation for the operation got underway, the injections were administered and my father was now asleep. We did not know if he would ever open his eyes again, but this was never talked about. He was alive and we were clinging to this, as you would cling on to a log if you were drowning. Everything was out of our control now, and we could only hope and pray.

Things were quiet in our house that night. I forget who looked after us that evening, but I know my mother and Mog went back to the hospital, to await developments. The operation lasted several hours and the news was good. They managed to save his legs before the poison spread from the legs to the rest of the body. The surgeon could not be sure if he would ever walk again; strange as this may appear, it did not seem important, after what we had been through. He was alive and he would survive; that is all we cared about.

My father spent many months in hospital, there were several

other operations on his legs but his spirit was high. We felt as if we had come through the worst of the storm and had reached a haven at last. Each day that went by, my father grew stronger, still confined to bed, and unable to walk, but looking healthier every time I saw him.

There was not the slightest doubt in his mind that he would walk again.

"A collier I am bloody staying, when I am out of this place. I will be walking to work again and back in the garden. You all wait and see," he informed all the visitors at his bedside. They all laughed and said that if anyone will do it, it would be Dai. Not one of the visitors believed it, to judge from the conversation on the way home, but my father believed it, and so did I.

Times were a lot harder than normal now. My father had not worked for several months, and there was no sign of him ever starting back. He was still in hospital and would be there for a while yet. The only income coming into our house was the small amount of compensation from the pit. A better word would have been, pittance allowance; the amount was so small. I often wondered how my mother could make ends meet. The reality of the situation was that we were constantly without money; every penny was spent on food.

There was not enough over to pay the mortgage, or the insurances, so they would have to wait. Times were hard indeed, but I cannot remember ever going hungry. My mother made sure there was food on the table, going without herself, leaving the food for us to eat. She never complained once about our lack of money. As long as she had "Dai," she would manage. She would moan about everything else though; her fiery spirit was firmly back.

She would take charity from no one. It was her family and she would manage, come hell or high water. We were now firmly back on dry land. My mother was stubborn as ever and the dust had better look out. Lol was back and in control.

None of the valley people had a lot, so, for us, having less was no great hardship. There was no keeping up with the Joneses in those days. There were too many Joneses for that to be a problem. Half the valley was somehow related to a Jones at some time. The valley people kept true to type, and the spirit of companionship, help, and solidarity, for one of their own who was in trouble, shone through.

The neighbours would rally round and help, not in a sense of giving and showing how good they were, but in a sense of true compassion for one of their own kind, in the only way a mining community would know how. If my mother thought for even a moment that the neighbours thought she was a charity case, all hell would break out.

I could hear her voice even now. "I am no one's bloody lackey. I take charity off no bugger, so don't even try."

Over the years, she helped and fought many battles with and for the neighbours, where she thought there was injustice and unfairness, and it was now the neighbours' chance to return the compliment to this proud, stubborn, determined woman, but this would not be easy. The neighbours were in and out of each other's houses at all hours, day and night, and there always seemed to be someone in our house, or my mother was in someone else's house. What they used to find to talk about I did not know, but talk they did.

"Thirteen to the dozen and a few dozen more," my father used to say, but I never understood what this meant.

This coming and going of neighbours would be out of character in today's world. An appointment must be made before we would call on a friend, telephoning beforehand to see if it is still convenient. In those days, the only appointment you would make would be with the doctor, and this would be avoided at all costs.

My father could not attend to the garden that year. I could not do it because I was too young; it was dug and planted by uncle Mog; who also had his own garden to tend. The only allusion to this act of kindness was Mog saying to my mother,"I hope Dai will not mind, but I was looking for and needed something to do, to pass the time and to keep me out of the pub. I have been drinking too much lately. If you see him before me, could you ask if he could do me this favour and let me spend a few hours in his garden? Dai could really help me out here."

These few hours developed into him completing work in the whole garden and making sure we had fresh vegetables that year. This act of kindness was not mentioned again, the garden was quietly looked after by Mog, who gave the impression that my father was doing him a favour.

My mother enjoyed her packet of fags.

"My one little luxury," she used to tell me.

In those days, everyone seemed to smoke. Often, when the neighbours were around, which was all the time, they always offered my mother cigarettes. Frequently, when it was my mother's turn to offer, they declined, pretending they were not ready for another cigarette. This act epitomises the way the Valley valued one of their own. My mother got pleasure from her cigarettes, and used to inhale the smoke deeply into her lungs, unaware of the dangers of this weed.

Our house would be full of smoke; any small room with a few people in it would be the same. The ceiling was stained brown with the nicotine, but they were happy, it was their enjoyment and a way to relax and get away from the everyday worries of the life they were forced to live in the name of progress.

Neighbours would turn up with a cake newly baked, or a tureen of broth, making the excuses that they had made too much, and it will go off if not eaten, and could the boys finish it off as a favour? No one liked waste, especially food, and we obliged with great gusto. Broth was our favourite food, made with good, solid vegetables and meat, all boiled together and strained before eating. I can smell it now, and it brings a warm feeling to the stomach.

Other members of the family called: Nan, my mother's sister from Tonyrefail, and Doug, her husband, who together kept the Red Cow Public House in that town. Often, when they arrived, there would be something for us. Pies and crisps were our favourites.

"Come on, boys, tuck in, there is plenty here. They will only go waste," Nan would announce in high voice. "There are also a couple of bottles of pop in the car. Run out and get them, will you."

A few bottles of beer would already have been smuggled past the hospital staff, before they arrived. I suspect the nurses knew exactly what was happening but turned a blind eye.

The number of times Mog left an almost full packet of cigarettes on the chair, just before leaving, are more than I can remember, but it happened often. The next time he visited, my mother would comment on the cigarettes and hand them back to him, only to hear him say, "Ho, there they are. I bought a new packet. You have these."

My mother would protest; Mog would insist, indignation in his voice.

"What the bloody hell do you think I am? I have one packet, and that is enough for me. Stop trying to bloody kill me by making me smoke myself to death." Mog knew exactly what he was doing, and so did my mother, both proud people, but one needed help and the other gave it in a spirit of love, each too proud to admit it. What a stubborn lot they were, right to the end!

Davy, the youngest of the brothers, would always be on hand and would always know when thing were difficult, frequently helping in more ways than I am able to remember. We all pulled together in one way or another, helping when help was needed, keeping out of the way when things were going all right. Facing the world together, with not much in the way of material wealth between them all, they were wealthy in other ways, the right ways, staying together, working as one unit, but respecting the pride and individuality of each other.

The time was coming when my father was due out of hospital. Brush in hand, my mother was determined to arrest any speck of dust found in the house, and immediately punished the culprits by throwing them into the fire. This was her way of warning all other stray specks of dust that were harbouring an inclination to enter our house.

"Dai is coming home, he will enter a clean house."

She was happy and laughing, warning us to keep the house clean and to not make a noise when he is home.

"I'll knock your bloody blocks off and you'll walk about headless, and then try and make a noise. There is to be no noise when your father is home. Do you all hear what I am saying?"

"Yes, mam," we quickly replied. All warnings from my mother were taken seriously, if you knew what was good for you, and we were no exception to this rule. I wondered if this rule would also apply to her, because she made the most noise. This thought brought a smile to my face, when I imagined her trying to knock her own head off, but I dared not risk saying a word.

We were all excited about having our father back. The hospital had had him long enough.

"He belongs at home," my mother said, "and home he shall come. I will look after him now. My Dai is coming home."

If she said these words once, she repeated them ten times more. My mother was happy with the type of happiness you can only feel when you are deeply in love with another human being. My parents were soul-mates, lovers and friends, and he was coming home. They had been through a lot together, and their troubles only helped to strengthen their affection for each other. If everything was pronounced all right, after the doctor's visit tomorrow, he could be released at two in the afternoon.

The doctor signed him out of the hospital. The ambulance arrived early afternoon, and out came my father, looking frail, but we did not care. The wheelchair was placed outside the ambulance door, and my father was carried out and placed into it. The distance to our door was only a few metres from the ambulance but, before the wheelchair arrived at the front door, my father asked the ambulance driver to stop, "I will walk through the door. Stop."

This horrified my mother, and she ordered the driver to push him into the house and to not to take any notice of him. She really went over the top. My father looked at her, and, in a slow, clear voice, said, "I said stop, I will walk through my own front door. Lol, give me help to get out of the chair."

I expected my mother to refuse. To my amazement, there was not a word spoken. She helped him to his feet, let his hand go, and my father, his legs still weak, walked through his own door. The wheelchair was behind him, and he sat back into it, happy. My father was home and, against all the odds, walking.

Still short of money, everyone doing his or her bit to help, the days passed into weeks, weeks into months; each one the same as the last. We were happy together, and I had another birthday.

My youngest brother was now into everything; all my toys were either sucked and wet, or pulled apart in the advancement of science. My mother was always busy, and my father started to get about the house and go for short walks. Mog would turn up and ask,"Fancy a short stroll, Dai? The weather will be fine today."

"You will have to walk slowly. I am still a bit unsteady, Mog."

"That is no problem. How about half an hour's walking, to get us in the mood for a pint of beer?"

We were a family enjoying the experience of being together, in high spirits, and satisfied that we were all in good health. On one of these short strolls, when I was accompanying my father, we walked up to the top of the street and sat down on a bench, aware of the sounds of the pit in the background but not hearing the noise directly. It seemed part of the echo in the air. We were born with this clatter and, in a strange sort of way it seemed a part of the valley, as if the sounds were natural. We were born into the hurley burley of the valley, with all its noises reverberating around us. These sounds gave the impression that they had a right to be there; they had become part of the valley.

We were sitting quietly, and my father said to me, "You know you must never go down the pit. Do not follow in my footsteps. The pit is not for you."

I had never thought about work, and when I did, it seemed natural that I would end up in the pit. All the people I valued in the world worked in the pit. If it was good enough for them, why should I be any different? I kept quiet and waited for him to continue.

There were several pits between Treorchy and Cwmparc, and everyone I knew worked in the pit. There were buses to and from our street every fifteen minutes. The place was always filled with people going to or coming from work, a constant stream of people running to catch their bus, or getting off the bus to start their shift, lunch box under arm.

The whole place was busy. The Tremains was full in the daytime and especially when shifts were due to change. It was our way of life and it seemed as if it would go on forever more. My grandfathers and great-grandfathers had all worked in the pit. What did my father expect me to do?

He had first hand experience of how the people of the Valley were destroyed, crippled, choked, broken into pieces and left to cough to death in pursuit of coal. He did not wish this life for me.

"It will be over my dead body, when I allow you to go to work in the pit," he forcefully informed me, in a way that brooked no argument.

Jim, my father's cousin, joined us on the seat. He also had a brother, Jim, living across the road in number twelve, the house where his parents once lived, and where he was born and brought up. Jim, his cousin, was older than my father and lived a few doors up from our house, in the same block. He worked on the winder as a watcher, unable to carry out any heavy duties because he had broken his back in the pit when he was young.

He could get about with a stick, but his back was always bent right over. I used to feel like asking my mother to place him on the ironing board and iron him straight. He would need a lot of steam, I thought, and my mother would have to press hard to make any impression. His stoop was quite pronounced, and he looked as if he should be walking on four legs, not two. His hands were practically touching the floor. There was a comical aspect about the way he would move around, stick in hand, and pipe in mouth, going about his every day business. He would never need to sit down to go to the toilet, I thought; he would be on permanent standby, ready for action whenever the eventuality would arise.

My father was a fluent Welsh speaker, and reverted to Welsh when his family got together. He spoke Welsh to Jim.

"How are you, Dai," Jim asked.

"Ho, I am so and so," my father replied. So and so meant all was well, could be better, but I am not worried.

"When will you be ready to go back to work?"

"I am ready now, but the doctor will not sign me off."

"I think the doctor is right, you know, Dai," Jim said, as if he possessed a secret knowledge of the medical profession.

"Well, I am feeling alright in myself, and could go back to light duties."

"You know what is best, but, mark my words, if you fall ill again, I'll be visiting you five feet under, and bringing flowers to place over you."

"I don't need your flowers, Jim. They are better left in the garden, not over me in the cemetery. Flowers are for life and to be looked at and admired. They are not for the dead."

They both laughed at this remark, pipes in mouths, and carried on puffing, holding the stems in a similar manner, as if copying each other. One puffed; the other puffed; like two steam trains chugging along side by side, smoke twirling around their heads, looking around, saying nothing, enjoying the smoke.

After a while, the conversation would start up again.

"How is the misses down there? I often hear her in the garden, when I am in the toilet, but have not seen her for a while."

"She is fine. If it was not for her, during the last few months, you would be putting flowers on me, Jim. I would have been long gone."

"Aye, she is a good one; a bit fiery, mind you, Dai, but her heart is in the right place."

"A bit fiery? A bloody lot fiery," my father replied. "She is like a bull in a china shop when she has something on her mind, a bull with no respect for the china."

They both nodded, as if they shared some knowledge of the working of my mother's mind and were complimenting each other on it. They had known each other all their lives, and went back a long way as friends. My father remembered the day Jim broke his back underground. A log he was fixing slipped and knocked him to the ground, trapping him to the floor. Part of the roof fell on his back and broke his spine. He was in bed for years, but regained partial use of his legs, and was able to walk but with difficulty. Since that time, he was given light duties on the top of the pit, and then worked as a watcher in the winding house.

Chapter 7

MY FATHER'S CONTINUED to improve until he was back to his old self, looking strong and healthy. He was now practically living outdoors, only coming in at meal times. It had been a long struggle to survive without the weekly wage packet, but he was ready to take his place back at the pit and start work; it would be light duties for the first few months and then back to his old job.

"Why do you go down the black hole? You are well now. It was the hole that made you ill. Do not go back, Daddy; there must be other jobs you can do," I remember saying to him.

"Things are what they are, my boy; what must be, must be. The colliery is my way, it has always been my way, and it is too late for me to be different. You are the one who must break the mould and not go down the pit."

"But what if I feel the pit is the right way for me?" I replied tentatively, knowing my father had strong views against letting me go into the pit.

"There is a right way and a wrong way to grow up and take your place in the world, but the pit is wrong for you. I want you to go forward, and carve out a better life for yourself."

He spoke slowly, with emotion in his voice. I was immensely proud of my father, and if I could carve out for myself his values, and grow up to be like him, I would feel this would be my right way. I did not say how I felt, because I could feel the strength of feeling against letting me go into the pit.

We stopped speaking for a while, and then he looked at me sternly.

"Do not chase an empty rainbow only to get a soaking, and

believe me when I tell you, the pit is the wrong way for you."

"How will I know the right way?" I asked, wondering why he was so strongly against the pit for me and why it was my wrong way.

"How does a bird know to fly south for the winter?"

"By instinct," I answered quickly, without thought.

"Follow your intuition, and you will know," he said. "I am no longer ill, we need the wage packet, your mother has been marvellous, and my friends have been good, but it is time to work. To stay from work now that I am well is a betrayal of the people that have helped us, including your mother, and that is not my way."

The following week, my father started back to work.

At about this time, we had a new neighbour across the road from us in my grandparents' old house. Jim, my father's brother, was still living there, the only brother that had not married and moved on. He was living alone now and had decided to take in a lodger and a housekeeper.

They were known to my family before.

"They are from good, solid stock," I once heard my parents say of them. They only lived down the road, in the next block, but the space there was restricted. There were already several people living in the house, and this seemed a good idea for all parties. Jim would get someone to look after him and the house, and they would have a roof over their heads and more space.

They quickly became close friends of our family, and we boys used to refer to them as uncle and aunt. A bond had developed between the two families and was kept until my parents died. They were devoted and trustworthy family friends. My mother wouldn't hear a word said against them; indeed, if there was so much as a rumour against them she would immediately put the offending party right, and when my mother put someone right, there was no margin of doubt. They used to be back and forth between each other's houses many times each day. This is how they were, not really relying on each other for anything, yet, in a strange sort of way, they came to rely totally on each other. They shared a lot of feelings and emotions.

Mair was that rare breed of woman with a natural mothering instinct; an old mother hen springs to mind. Crossing the road to number twelve would mean sweets or a drink or both; you were guaranteed at least a biscuit, if nothing else. Nothing seemed too much trouble for her, as far as we were concerned; we were definitely under her wing. If we misbehaved, the old mother hen was no shrinking violet when it came to putting you in your place. She would cluck and sit on us like a hen sits on her eggs, keeping a tight reign on us, but still keeping us warm, to show she cared. She would also protect us. She was a formidable lady with a heart as beautiful as the morning sun. She was a bit hot at times, but only when the need arose. It was no wonder that Mair and my mother got along so well together and were such close and true friends.

Mair's husband, Glyn, was not as forward, in fact, not forward at all, but always in the background, in a gentle helpful way, whenever needed. He would always be in the right place at the right time. He was the type of person you would wish to have on your side, but cannot put your finger on exactly why.

My mother always had a lot of time for Glyn, a lot more than for Jim. There was always uneasiness between the two. They often did not see eye to eye; my mother thought he was a tight old skinflint, and would have told him so, tactfulness being her Achilles' heel.

"He would skin a flea for a farthing," she once told my father.

They used to keep out of each other's way whenever possible, but, where this was not the case, my father often told her to hold her mouth. I don't know why he used to bother. He would have had more success asking the dog not to bark when hungry. To ask my mother to hold anything she did not wish to hold would be a feat that Hercules would find difficult. Her mouth would open and out would come her thoughts. My mother was convinced Jim was a total taker, giving nothing in return. This infuriated her and a full-blown argument between the two usually followed. Mutual avoidance would always be the preferred option.

"He is my brother, after all," my father would protest.

"The reason he never married is because he is so bloody cold-hearted. The only thing in his life he kisses is the pint glass down the Park Hotel. You know I am telling the truth, don't you, Dai?"

"He is still my brother; now come on, Reen, be a bit more accommodating."

When my father called her Reen instead of Lol he was after agreement, and she would respond with:

"I'll do my best."

Her best would be to carry on as before, but she said the right thing, and my father would be satisfied.

Chapter 8

TO THE RIGHT of our field, on the hillside and further up the mountain, my father owned another plot of ground, in partnership with his friend Huey. There were several long sheds there, built by the two of them for rearing chickens from eggs. They kept a few hundred chickens and surplus eggs were sold all round Cwmparc. There was a stream running the length of the garden, and the top end was dammed to form a duck pond for ducks and a few geese. "The guardians of the garden," my father called the geese.

They used to take it in turns to feed the chickens, before starting work on the early shift, which began at six o clock in the morning. They were up and out by five o'clock in the morning, to finish the task before the working day began, and in all types of weather. When working different shifts, they would cover for each other, in seeing to the chickens.

Each night, the chicken sheds had to be locked up and secured against foxes. Sometimes, this would be down to Brian, the youngest son of Huey, and me to perform. It was drummed into us that to do it incorrectly would mean the loss of every chicken.

"The fox does not kill one chicken and take it for food," my father said. "This carnivore would kill every one, if not disturbed, and leave the chicken shed before the break of day. The fox is a highly trained killing machine, and would kill a whole pen of chickens in a few minutes."

My father showed not the slightest malice towards the fox, but he made it clear that we were not to be excused laziness.

"It is their nature to be what they are. If we do not protect the birds against this opportunist, it is our fault, not the fox's, when we lose the lot."

Sometimes, Brian and I went in the garden, generally messing about in the stream at the back of the chicken sheds. We would dam the water up in different places and paddle in it. We used stones, clods of earth, and old wood to hold the water back, and anything else we could find to form the dam. It was fun, and often we would catch fish from the larger river nearby and release them into these ponds. We were always covered in mud and dirt; our fingernails could have fed an army of germs. The dirt would be ingrained into our hands, but we were oblivious to it. Even if we noticed, I don't think we would have been troubled in the least. We were young and carefree in a harsh world; we would take our fun where we could.

Once, on account of our superior hunting skills, we decided to go stalking rats in the undergrowth at the edge of the garden, where there was a bramble hedge intertwined with nettles and various trees. We practised beforehand with the new slug gun Brian had recently acquired, which we believed would enhance these superior hunting skills further. Rusty old tins were placed at one end of the garden, and for about an hour, we practised hitting these with the slug pellets. We were now equipped to attack anything that moved in the garden.

Dead Eye Thomas and I believed that, if the rats had any sense, they would stay quiet or move to another garden, and so we went stalking in smug satisfaction. We were the Rambos of Cwmparc, rat catchers, and destroyers of vermin extraordinaire. To enhance our image as serious rat exterminators, we wore caps on our heads. We each had a knife in our belts and looked every inch, or so we thought, marauding huntsmen.

We stayed back from the hedge, watching for any movement, the gun at the ready. Nothing stirred. We waited, like two tigers, ready to strike at the next thing to move. Still nothing moved, so we decided to beat the hedge with a stick, reasoning that we would disturb anything hiding in the undergrowth. We saw movement in the undergrowth; our direct attack was paying off. The vermin were being flushed out. I shouted to Brian to be ready.

"There is something in the nettles. Prepare yourself."

Brian fired into the dark interior, the bushes moved, there was a clatter and a lot of clambering in the hedge. We had got one.

We both ran over, feeling elated and excited about the way we had handled the situation. When we moved the nettles, horror struck us both. We looked at each other, and then at the floor, back into the hedge, down to the floor, and both uttered the same words simultaneously.

"Oh, shit! We're in for it now."

At our feet, its wings stretched, not moving, was a cockerel. We had shot a cockerel, and to compound the situation, it was not any old cockerel, it was one of my father's prize breeding birds. Our superior hunting skills left us immediately. We were in deep trouble now. How could we explain this? Could we say we thought the cockerel was a rat in the undergrowth? Our parents would never buy it.

I could only say, "Ho, ho, we are in for it now; ho, ho, we are in for in now." Brian said, "Let's pretend we never did it."

We need a better plan than this, I thought. Who else would shoot a cockerel in our own garden, and with a slug gun? Things were getting desperate; we needed a plan, any plan. We were in it up to our necks.

We sat on the ground, stunned, watching the lifeless cockerel.

"We could say the fox had him," I suggested, looking for some hope in my friend's eyes.

"We are responsible for the chickens. How can we say this?" he asked.

"Let's pretend the cockerel ran away." I suggested.

"I'll help him to pack," Brian said sarcastically.

We were now in a state of panic. We needed answers, and we needed them quickly, or we were for the high jump with a very heavy landing.

We thought it best to come clean with our fathers, tell them the whole story and hope they would understand. We dreaded the telling but felt we had run out of options. To try and mitigate the crime somewhat, we thought we would feather the bird, clean out the inside, present it as a *fait accompli*, apologize and hope for the best. We knew we were in for a row but at least we were behaving responsibly, or so we thought.

We tied the feet together, hung the bird upside down on a spike and I started to feather it. This was warm work, the pressure was getting to us, and we decided to take a rest and cool off in the stream. The time spent cooling off developed into about an hour. We were trying to delay the inevitable for as long as possible, before we completed the task and faced our parents.

We returned to the bird, expecting to see him still hanging on the hook, but he was gone.

"Where is the cockerel, Brian?" I shouted.

We looked at each other in silent amazement.

"Dead cockerels are not supposed to run away?" Brian remarked.

Looking around the garden, we found the answer. The bird was alive; feet still tied, hopping around mad, half plucked, and not at all happy with his lot. The slug pellet had only stunned the bird. There was another problem now: how do we give him back his feathers?

We decided to catch the bird, untie his legs, let him roam in the field and hope for the best. Our parents need never know; we were safe. Just to be extra sure, I mentioned to my father that the cockerel had been fighting and there were feathers all over the garden. That is how we both got away with the matter of the cockerel.

Chapter 9

MY YOUNGER BROTHER was crawling and into everything; anything left on the floor was sucked, pulled, sat on, or broken. He was a right little pain, but he was our brother and we loved him. From our house to the back garden were a number of steps, and we had always to be on our guard against the baby falling down them. Once, when we were not as diligent as we should have been, we suddenly spotted him at the top of the steps, looking over and preparing to fly over the edge.

My mother turned red in the face, then white with shock. She slowly walked to the steps, so as to not alarm the baby, and grabbed him by the leg. If he had fallen down the steps it could have killed him. After this, a gate was fitted and kept closed at all times, to keep the little pain out of mischief. He would move across the floor in the wink of an eye, and had to be watched at all times. If I could avoid him I would, but he seemed to be everywhere.

I was too young to baby-sit, and Mair came over to look after us when my parents wished to go out together. On these occasions, her brother Davy and his wife Peg would call up from Chepstow with their new car, and they would all go out dancing in Treorchy, at the EMI club. These events would be eagerly awaited, and as Saturday night approached, the excitement grew. My parents would be collected at about seven in the evening, and from five o'clock onwards, my mother would be washing her hair, cleaning her nails, painting her face, looking in the mirror and commenting about her earrings and the shape of her nose. All the while, she kept asking us how she looked, and was never happy when we told her.

"Dai," she would bellow, "What do you think of this dress?"

"You look very smart, Reen," he would answer, without even looking up, knowing what the next question would be.

"Why do you like this dress?" she would insist, as if trying to start an argument.

My father's response would usually be, "Ask Davy; he will tell you the same. We all like that dress."

This would satisfy my mother and she would stop asking. An hour later, she would be ready. Dave and Peg would arrive; my father, who up until now, had been be sitting down, smoking his pipe, would start getting ready. He would get his coat, shout he is ready and say, "Come on, Reen, I am waiting for you."

My mother would grumble, "You cannot go out like that, Dai. Go and get changed."

"I wouldn't get changed if you were the bloody Queen. My clothes are clean and tidy, so there."

"All right then, Dai," she would say, and away they would go to the dancing.

The garden was still a central part of my life, and the shed we owned in the large field needed to be enlarged to accommodate a new calf we were to purchase. My father planned the height of the shed sides and the size of the roof angle, which was to slope down at the same angle as the near by house roofs: forty-five degrees. The walls of the cowshed were constructed of upright railway sleepers. My father had purchased a job lot from the railway, a few months earlier, and had tarred them a few times, to help protect the timber against the weather. We dug the foundations, mixed the cement and placed the railway sleepers upright into holes filled with cement, holding the uprights in place by cross bars until the cement dried. The upright sleepers were further strengthened by a number of cross sleepers, and the whole structure was bolted together through holes already drilled, the whole forming a secure upright structure.

The cross bars and roof supports were made of recycled wood from the pit and cut to length by us. They were placed upright on top of the sleepers at the correct angle, and sealed into a roof-tree that ran the full length of the construction. The whole structure was nailed or bolted together, to form a solid wooden framework, to which the panel boards were nailed. These cross panels were placed at four foot intervals, and covered the whole of the framework. Across the angles, wooden boards were nailed, locking the whole structure together.

These boards were four feet long and a foot wide, and were originally ammunition boxes, purchased from the army. We dismantled these boxes and used the timber for all manner of jobs. The top of the cowshed was completely covered with these boards, securely nailed into the wooden cross sections. Over these boards and across the upright sleepers was thick belting, recycled from the slag heaps. The strips were conveyer belts used to transport coal, underground and on pit surface. The belts were frequently changed and the old belts discarded onto the slag heaps. These were what we fetched, cleaned and nailed over the wooden structure of the cowshed.

Pitch was heated up in a large drum, over an open fire, and the hot liquid was painted over the surface, sealing the nail holes and forming a thick coating over the belting; waterproofing the inside of the cowshed against the elements.

The inside of the shed walls was whitewashed with lime to make the interior light and to protect the timber against wood rot and lice. The floor was cemented and had drainage holes placed around the edges and in the centre, at a slight angle, to allow for easy drainage.

Every weekend and most evenings, when my father was working the day shift, we would be there. Occasionally, Mog would turn up to help us for a while, and then he went away, to walk the mountain. He always asked if I was coming with him, but I usually stayed, to help complete the work. It was not easy but I enjoyed every minute of it. I would be up on the roof, nailing in the boards, hitting home every nail with pride and confidence, trying to demonstrate that I was grown up and able to do my share.

I held the pit belting as my father skilfully rammed home the larger nails. The satisfaction I experienced over these few weeks cannot be expressed by words alone. There is something uplifting when a father and son are able to work together in harmony at a common task.

The building of the cowshed seemed to take up all our free time. We were organizing the wood, achieving and constructing together; it just seemed natural and as if it would always be this way. Looking back, this work meant more to me than I realised. I did not appreciate the importance of sharing time with someone I loved and respected, until that person was no longer around.

My father was poor, uneducated in the conventional sense, and would not stand out in a crowd but he taught me about life, the importance of hard honest work, the correct way to live, and the significance of spending time with people you care about, before it is too late. This period stays in my mind because we were always together and shared the four most precious gifts a father and son are able to share, *our time, love, thoughts and values.* What a lucky person I was, to have had a person of this quality as my father. I was experiencing the most important gift a son could share with his father, and was too young and in-experienced to fully understand it at the time. How privileged I now feel, when I look back, with the wisdom of age, at the time we built the cowshed together.

Chapter 10

O N A TUESDAY, my father and a few of his friends sometimes went to the cattle market at Bridgend, utilising rest days from the colliery; he was entitled to about six per year. These outings were a real treat and would be looked forward to. On this particular occasion, my father and four of his friends had planned to go to the market and were eagerly waiting the day. There was Jim Watkins, Ron Evans, and two other people, whose names escape me. Ron was the only one who could drive. He owned an old Morris Minor that he had painted blue, to hide the rust.

The day arrived and Ron turned up at eight o clock to pick up my father. The rest of the quartet was already in the car, and it was full. I thought there would be no room left for my father. The car was small, and the four people already squashed into it looked like giants. They had to make room for my father. This had all the makings of a disastrous day. To see three adults, one over twenty stone, in the back of a Morris Minor car is some experience. The tyres looked as if they were about to burst; at the least, they looked as if they would never stay inflated as far as Bridgend. The whole scene gave the impression of something out of the Key Stone Cops.

They were just about to pull off when my father shouted, "Have we got room for the boy?"

Room! I thought, they would have difficulty in breathing in that space, let alone find room for me.

"Plenty of room," they shouted. "Get in. Come on, hurry up."

Ron gesticulated and ordered me to get into the car.

"Get in where?" I asked, looking all perplexed.

"Get into the back. There is more than enough room. Be sharp, or we will leave you behind."

Jim Watkins, rather agitated because I was delaying them by not getting into the car, shouted at me to hurry. My mother came to the door, to see what all the commotion was all about, and before she could say a word, I excitedly shouted, "They have asked me to go to the market with them. Can I please go, mammy?"

She looked at the car and the occupants, smiled in a disbelieving way, and remarked, laughing, "If you are able to get into that car, you deserve to go," she said. "Be gone with you." She pushed me towards the car door.

I squeezed in the back and sat on the floor, against the side of the back window, with not an inch of room to move, and off the car went, with us looking like a tin of sardines, moving down Cwmparc.

We had been on the road for no more than twenty minutes, when one of the sardines shouted, "Stop the car. I need the toilet. Hurry up. I can't wait."

The car pulled into the next lay-by and stopped. The two front passengers got out. I was handed over from the back, in the same way as you would hand over a sack of potatoes.

"Be careful of the boy. I don't want him damaged," my father jokingly remarked.

The front seat was pulled forward and no one moved. They were all jammed in, stuck solid.

"Give us a hand; we can't move," Jim shouted, red in the face.

"Here, grab my hand, Dai," Ron said, and he and the other passenger in the front held their hands out for my father to grab hold of and pull, in order to dislodge himself from the back. The two other sardines were given the same treatment and they, too, were free.

"There is more room in the two foot nine at the pit, than in the back of this car," my father remarked, referring to the height of the coal seam he was working underground. He lit his pipe to catch a quick smoke.

There were a few trees near the lay-by, and each man marched to a different tree. A few moments later, the four of them stood next to their chosen tree, a few groans and moans could be heard as they unbuttoned the fronts of their trousers, and then silence, as if in reverence to the sound of gushing water; giving the tree a pressure shower that I am sure it was not enjoying in the slightest. The shower completed, I watched as they returned. One weighed at least twenty stone, the other two about sixteen stone, with my father and Ron about twelve stone, all heading back to the little blue car. Poor car, I thought, with all this weight, it will never take us to the market. Even if it gets us there, to expect it to take us home again would be too much. The rest of the party started to squash into the small interior. This was a sight to watch, bottoms and stomachs all fighting to be accommodated in a space far too small for them. They were going to the market and, one way or another, they intended to get there.

We stopped again on the way, Ron affectionately commenting, "The old girl is getting too warm; she needs a drink and a rest."

The car was overheating, smoke was billowing out from under the bonnet and the engine was rasping as if in pain. Ron knew exactly what the problem was. He went to the boot of the car and pulled out a large can of water, waited for about fifteen minutes for the engine to cool down, opened the bonnet, unscrewed the radiator cap and poured the contents of the can into the radiator.

"This will make you feel better," he said, talking to the car as if it were human. "You will be alright now."

He was beaming and tapping the top of the car at the same

time. The rest nodded in agreement, and one of them remarked laughingly,

"She is a good old girl."

The car arrived at the market thirty minutes later. The car park was almost full when we arrived, but we parked the car with little trouble. The same procedure as happened earlier had to be adopted again, in order to get everyone out of the car, and away we trooped into the market.

The market was arranged in sections, one section for each of the different types of animals for sale. The sheep section consisted of low, interlocking pens, inside each of which were the different breeds of sheep, in lots ranging from one to about ten. The pig section was similar but the pens were a lot sturdier and heavier, more permanent than the sheep pens. The main cattle sector was indoors, with a few sections outside, all full of cattle of all types and colours. The chicken quarter consisted of a number of cages stacked on the floor, with further cages placed on top. Various other animals were dotted about in the market, all with the individual owner's name stamped on them, ready for the sale.

The hustle and bustle of the market could be heard everywhere. People were milling around the enclosure, into and out of the market yard and pens, deliveries of new livestock were constant, cattle trucks and animal carriers were all over the place. The whole scene seemed disorganised, with everybody going their own way and doing their own thing. The noise penetrated every corner of the area. Cattle, sheep, pigs, chickens and ducks combined in one continuous noise, augmented by the shouting of the farmers and buyers.

Men of all shapes and sizes, some with sticks in their hands, were walking round the animal pens, and wearing clothes that would be an insult in a jumble sale, looking, touching and commenting on the various animals in the enclosures. Most men had flat caps on their heads, Wellington boots on their feet, and a wide leather belt round their middles, pulled tight over a lump that was expensively purchased with beer. No one cared how they looked or what any one thought; they were there to sell, buy, or just look, but, mainly, they would all have a good time.

Into this arena we arrived.

"Let's take a look at the horses," Jim Watkins proposed.

"In a minute; there is plenty of time; we have all day," my father replied.

We walked around the market; commented on a few things; prodded a few animals; spent a bit of time looking at the cattle and horses.

"This is a fine mare; just look at those teeth, Ron," Jim said loudly, making sure his knowledge of horses would be heard by anyone near. My father discussed with a few old friends the attributes of the market and how expensive everything seemed. I listened to the auctioneers warming up for the day's business and planning the different animal lots for sale as Ron commented,"This is warm work, Dai."

They all nodded their heads in agreement. Watching all these activities would make any full-blooded male thirsty, and they were already at the limit of their endurance.

"Let's go across the road for a quick pint," Jim suggested, knowing the rest of the group would be in full agreement. A visit to the liquid trough now became essential. Marketing is thirsty work, and to quench this marketing thirst, the answer could only be found in the market's watering hole.

"What about the boy?" Ron asked, looking at me and smiling so that I would not feel that I was a problem.

"Leave him outside. He will be alright with crisps and lemonade," my father remarked, and they left me, returning a few minutes later with crisps and lemonade as a peace offering to keep me quiet.

The market pub was open all day, from ten in the morning until late into the night. Every room inside was full to capacity and there were always several people standing by the door, waiting to get into the establishment. Looking through the window from the outside, I could see the bar was full of customers waiting to be served, all pushing past each other as if their very lives depended upon it. Each person was trying to be served first. It was always done in a friendly manner; there was never any trouble or bad behaviour.

I could see my father and the rest of the party in the corner of the room, all talking, with pints in their hands, either smoking pipes or cigarettes. The beer was flowing well and the short trip to the bar for a refill was frequently repeated. The day would be spent one third in the market and two thirds at the watering hole. The hole seemed to be the most important part of the day, and an essential part of the plan, though no one seemed to acknowledge this point. From where I was situated, they seemed to spend more time going to and from the toilet than in the market, and it seemed strange to me, that a day at the market also meant so many visits to the toilet.

It was now approaching lunchtime, and the whole party decided to take another look round the market. My father wished to price newborn calves. I was full, and felt like a bubble about to burst. I was already into double figures with packets of crisps and lemonade.

"Come on, you lot, push past, we need to get back into the market." Jim shouted back to the other four as he came out the door.

"Let's look at the price of calves," my father said, as he emerged from the pub.

"I must have a sit down for a few minutes," one of the others moaned, "I have been standing all day." We all sat outside the pub for about ten minutes.

"Come on. Let's go, we have been here long enough," Ron said, standing up. The rest of us stood up, too, and walked over to the market.

The market was by now full, with barely room to walk around the different pens; the calf stalls were particularly busy.

"What is going on at the calf stalls? I have never seen the area this full before," Jim Watkins remarked.

"They are good value, and there are a lot of buyers looking for a bargain," a person next to Jim replied, making general conversation.

"Going cheap, hey?" my father chipped in, rubbing his chin. "Let's take a closer look." He pushed his way through to the front.

The auctioneers were busy selling calf after calf. A farmer standing next to my father remarked, "Now is the time to buy, get in quick," as he purchased a job lot of six calves. The next sale was a black and white Friesian calf, a few weeks old, and this is precisely what my father did. A few bids later, he was the new owner.

The rest of the group pushed forward to take a closer look at the calf, excitement showing in their eyes. Jim was the first to speak, "This calls for a celebration."

"Yes, we need to wet the calf's head," Ron exclaimed, and they all began walking in the direction of the pub.

"Hold on a minute, I need the toilet. I'll run round the back. The toilet in there will be full," Jim said. "Order me a pint of beer, and I'll catch you up later." He walked away and the others squeezed into the front door of the pub.

The celebration went on for a while; they were definitely feeling happy about the way the business went and the price they paid for the calf. I was still floating in past lemonade, and felt that, if any more of this liquid went down my throat, the bubbles would lift me up and float me home. The crisps I ate at the same time would help to hold me down, I reasoned, but there was no way I could handle any more lemonade.

"Here have this other drink and crisps," Jim offered, as he placed them on the bench and went back in side.

"No way," I thought, and tipped the lemonade down the nearby drain. I ate the crisps, reasoning that the more mouthfuls of the crisps I ate, the less chance there was of me floating away. This went on for most of the afternoon. More lemonade was poured down the drain; in the end, even the crisps went the same way, until the time arrived to collect the calf.

Out of the pub they all came, full to the brim with the liquid from the bar, the celebrations an obvious success, staggering to one side, correcting themselves and moving back to where they started. It was a puzzle to me how they were going to get the calf home. I had been puzzling about this from the time my father purchased the animal, but I reasoned that they were the adults and they must know what they were doing. There must be a plan and they were not telling me. I credited them with far too much intelligence, because they were grown up, and I was still a child. The quantity of beer that each man drank that day I am unable to state, but if a round equates to the volume of lemonade I drank, they were well into double figures.

Before we were allowed to collect the calf from the pen, my father went to the sales office to pay for his purchase. This was completed in a few minutes, and we all went over to collect the new arrival. I looked at the size of the calf, looked at the five boisterous men, all five sheets to the wind, giving the impression of being budding farmers but hardly able to stand straight, and envisaged the little Morris Minor and our journey here, and thought, "There is no way we have room for the calf."

We would have to walk the calf home, or tie it to the back of the car and hope it could keep up with us. The sales chit was handed to the sales checker at the pen, and the calf was in our ownership, led out by my father. It had a string around its neck, with the other end of the string firmly in my father's hand. "What now?" I thought.

Collecting the calf from the pen must have been hard work.

The first thing we did was to lead the animal across the road and tie it to a post near the entrance of the pub. My father said, "Look after the calf for a few minutes. We won't be too long."

The rest went inside, to recharge their liquid content. The celebrations were to continue, which seemed a waste because, no sooner did it go down one hole, but it came out a few minutes later at another. The calf was standing tied to the post, and I was by the side of it, stroking the animal and discussing with it how we would get home. The way the rest of the party was, I was getting more sense from the calf.

A while later, the party emerged, caps the wrong way round, singing and happy with being farmers for the day.

"Time to go home," Jim Watkins shouted. "Let's go home."

The group smiled, sang a few lines of, "I'm tired and I want to go to bed," and staggered over to the car. The only thing I could think about was how to get the calf home, and even if we managed this great feat, what would be the reaction of my mother? We walked over to the car, the calf walking behind and looking lost.

The boot of the car was opened and out came the can to fill the radiator. It was refilled from a nearby tap for the journey home. The calf would never fit into the boot. You would not get a chicken in there, let alone a calf; we were in trouble. The group looked at each other, scratched their heads, looked at the calf, back to the car, and Ron shouted, "Bloody Hell! Dai, how can we get this calf home?" Reality had finally set in; what now?

My father was not in the slightest ruffled.

"Now, now, Ron, we will sort this out. The animal is not very big."

He then went back into the market and returned a few minutes later with a large sack and a length of rope. We all looked on, wondering how the sack and the string would get the calf home. He cut four holes into the sack, had the calf lifted into the sack backwards, and placed the calf's legs one into each hole, and tied the open end of the sack around the calf's neck.

"This will stop the calf from moving around and causing trouble. It is all under control," he remarked.

Three of the party sat in the back of the car as before, and the calf was handed in over the front seats. The calf rested between the middle passenger's legs, with its head on his lap. The legs were tied together, to stop the animal from moving too much while in transit, and to protect it from kicking out.

"Get in here, and sit on my lap," my father told me. The plan seemed to be working.

The car moved off and we were on our way home, the calf quiet in the back, squashed into the sack and looking quite ridiculous. We had been travelling for fifteen minutes when there were shouts from the back.

"Stop, we all need to go to the toilet."

A minute later, Ron pulled in and stopped. I jumped out, followed by my father. The other three in the back could not move even an inch. What a sight they looked, three full-grown males, stuck solid, with the calf in the centre, all waiting to be helped out in order to go to the toilet.

"Hurry up, Dai, we are all desperate here," the party shouted impatiently.

The calf was handed out over the seats and placed on its side, by the road. The two front passengers tugged and pulled to dislodge the three stuck in the back.

The ablutions over, we were on our way again, the calf firmly back in the centre of the back seat. The old car was really straining.

"Come on, old girl, you can do it. Don't give out on us now," Ron coaxed, as the old car strained to move forward. The engine started to overheat again and we had to stop to fill the radiator with fresh water. The calf was handed over, then, after another twenty minutes, the trio needed the toilet again, and the pulling and tugging was repeated. The radiator filled and the engine cooled, we set off again on the homeward straight.

We were just starting on the mountain road over the valley when it happened. The calf opened its bowels. The smell was instantaneous, hitting us all in the back of the throat. The stink was of a sickly type, as if stale milk had been brought into the car and painted on our faces. It was foul and obnoxious, and seemed to hold in the car like a cloud, even though we opened all the windows. The first to speak was Jim, sitting with the calf between his legs.

"The mess is all over the floor and over my feet. Stop, Ron, or I will be sick. Hurry up."

The smell was getting worse, and then we heard the sound of water rushing, "Oh, no! Bloody hell!" howled the three in the back, as the calf passed enough water to soak the floor of the car front and back. I looked down and could see this fluid swishing around my feet, mixed with the white substance from the calf's bottom.

Ron was the first to speak.

"Dai, if you mention breathing through the mouth, I swear I'll rub your cap in the bloody stuff, followed by your nose."

My father looked round, kept his mouth firmly shut for a minute and then said, "It could be worse. It could have happened back in Bridgend."

By this time the car had come to a stop, windows wide open, with one of the party hanging his head out the window and being sick. This my father put down to smoking and drinking to much.

"You should not have drunk that last pint; it turned your stomach."

No mention was made of the foul smell; it looked as if my father would get away with it. We all got out of the car, the sack around the calf was wet and stained, the car wet and smelly, and one of the group heavily sick. He was now out of the car, face down by the side of the road, taking in the fresh air.

After a few minutes, the four looked at my father, looked at the car, and said in unison, "Dai, this was your bright idea. You bought the calf, now clean the car."

They sat down defiantly on the grass verge, waiting for the car to be cleaned.

"We are not touching the car until you have cleaned the floor," Ron bellowed, making sure my father understood the message.

He was given no choice. The car must be cleaned and there was only one person in the frame. The calf was cleaned first, with the grass from the mountain, and the sack removed and discarded under a nearby stone. My father went over to the car, bunches of grass in both hands, and started to clean the inside. He was at this task for over twenty minutes, fetching clean grass every minute or so. The last task was to place a blanket of grass over the floor. My father promised to clean the car with soap and water when we arrived home. We all got back into the car, the calf this time in the front with my father; I was squashed into the back. The car struggled to move forward, and after a lot of effort, we all arrived safely home.

The calf was taken to the cowshed and placed into a pen already prepared for it. The animal immediately lay down to rest on the straw, totally exhausted after the long journey. A dried milk substance was made up in a bucket and stirred. My father's two fingers were placed into the calf's mouth, and immediately the animal started to suck. The mouth of the calf was lowered to the bucket, and the liquid started to flow into the animal's mouth. The milk was sucked through my father's fingers, which were acting as a teat. After this, the calf settled down, and we went home for food and to suffer the wrath of my mother. My father could hardly stand and looked exhausted.

"What state is this to come home?" she remarked, in mock anger. "You are showing a bad example to the boy. You ought to be ashamed of yourself, do you hear me?" she ranted.

"I'm very ashamed," he stuttered, with a slight smile, and went straight up the stairs to bed. He was asleep in less than a minute.

That weekend, uncle Mog called over and, with walking stick in hand, announced, "I'm going walking. Are you joining me?"

Tramping the mountains was one of my greatest pleasures, and I immediately answered. "Of course I'm coming with you. Where are we going?"

"Just wait and see," he replied.

Sandwiches were made, together with a flask, and we were ready to set off for the day.

"We are going around the Ragged Mountain, following the Fishing River up to its source," he explained, not wishing to keep me in suspense any longer. All around our house and along the edge of the pit were the slag heaps, and the river near and all around the pit was black, stained with the waste and dust from the Black Hole. The water would once have been crystal clear, before the pits came to the valley, but it was now another casualty of Black Gold. Even the fish in the river could not hide from this foul dust. Part of the tip had moved with the rain over the years, and slid down into the bottom of the river, just above the pit. This resulted in the river running black, even before it ran past the colliery, where the pollution from the mine further damaged the water and sucked the life giving oxygen from it.

We did not linger by this part of the river, just walked past at a steady pace to the open, clear mountain above the valley floor. Thirty minutes walking and we were in the clear air; the river water was clear and the grass was green and alive, as nature intended.

"Breathe deep, feel the fresh air in your lungs, drink the God given air," Mog said. He would breath deeply, arms out-stretched, face into the wind, looking at the sky and showing me how I should fill my lungs and enjoy the clear fresh air. This meant so much to my uncle; he was at home walking the mountains, and wished me to share his enthusiasm and passion for nature and enjoy its natural delights.

We walked around the riverbanks, and Mog stopped from time to time, and looked for signs of badger tracks, fox tracks, and often came across a hedgehog hiding in the tall grass.

"Look at the different types of birds," he shouted, with wonderment in his eyes.

We watched them fly all around us, as we sat on the grass, trying to identify the different species. "What wonderful little creatures," he said, smiling heartily and pointing skyward.

After we had been walking for a few hours, we decided to stop for food. I had cheese and onion sandwiches, and Mog would have the same but without butter on his bread. Always, to finish the picnic, there would be an apple or orange and a cup of tea from the flask.

My uncle stopped, when we were walking along the river bank, and looked down at the flowing water.

"What do you hear?"

"Nothing," I replied.

"Listen closer to the water gurgling over the stones in the river bed. This is one of the most tranquil sounds you would ever wish to hear. There is something spiritual in the sound of running water. Just open your ears and listen."

"I can hear the sound," I replied.

Mog nodded and continued, "This sound will lift your spirit and calm your soul. Just listen; can you feel the water forming a spiritual bond with you? The sound of the water will bring you alive and let you bathe in the wondrous forces of its power. Just let it take hold and you will see."

Mog understood the environment and how to appreciate its beauty, long before the word environmentalist became fashionable. He stretched his arms above his head, sat on a large stone next to the flowing river, and added, "The water is speaking to you, telling you all is well, nature is alive and you are part of this living picture."

Profound words from my uncle, but as true now as they ever were. Mog was indeed an enigma, a chain-smoking, beer-swigging miner with a deep and profound understanding of nature and all its beauty, yet to meet him with his hammer would give you another impression.

After walking for a few more hours, we left the river for the mountainside, and decided to eat the rest of our sandwiches, then started back down to the river below. At the river's edge, Mog collected a pile of straw, bracken, leaves and wood, asked me to collect a number of large stones from the river bed and arrange them in a circle. He placed the material he had collected into the centre and lit a fire, added the wood a little later, and soon we had a roaring fire.

We removed our shirts, rolled up our trouser legs, and went into the river to fish. The conventional way to fish is with a rod, but there was no way we were able to get hold of one, so we used our hands; the method is known as fish tickling. Mog was in the water, hands under a stone.

"Always work up stream, with your body into the river flow, so the water runs past you, Find the most likely stone that a fish would hide under, look for the number of escape routes the fish can escape through, and if there are only one or two, that will be our target stone."

Only one stone in five had a fish or two under it, so a lot of time was spent searching with hands and fingers, only to find no occupants. We straddled the stone, felt under the water and searched until we were able to feel the cold scales of the trout. Slowly placing our fingers around the fish, moving our hands forward all the time, and little by little bringing the fish closer to the edge of the stone, until both hands were around the fish, with one quick movement, the fish would be thrown onto the bank.

We were at this task for nearly an hour and we caught three fish. They were about six to eight inches long, and we needed one more before we stopped. Mog shouted first.

"There is one in between my fingers. Quick! Place your hands by mine, ready to flick the fish onto the bank. It feels like a big one."

I placed both hands at the ready to cup the fish as it was brought out from beneath the stone. My hands closed on the fish, and, with a quick flick, I threw it onto the bank.

When I looked for it, there was no fish on the bank, but a great, fat, slimy toad, not very amused at having his siesta disturbed. It gave a few croaks, jumped and went back into the water. One more fish was still needed, and it took us another twenty minutes before we had our quota. I kept running back to the fire, to place more wood on it, in between the fish tickling.

The fish were skewered to a branch and placed above the fire, so that the smoke from the wood burning below would slowly cook them. We looked for a certain type of nettle that is quite common on the mountain, and at the base is a hard case. If this case is collected and roasted on the fire, the inside tastes similar to chestnuts. We collected about a dozen in a few minutes and placed them around the fire to roast. The feast was a success; we ate the fresh trout and the cooked nuts with the rest of our sandwiches; it was one of the best meals I ever experienced.

The food eaten, we rested a while, to digest it, lying on the grass, watching the fire burning lower into the ground.

Mog said, "Looking at the fire is sending me to sleep. Come, let's move."

We doused the fire with water collected from the river and carried in the empty tea flask, until it was totally extinguished. It was now late afternoon, and we carried on walking by the side of the river, the flow getting smaller as we got near to the source, under the Ragged Mountain. At last we arrived at the start of the river that would eventually become part of the River Taff and flow into the sea at Cardiff.

We sat down on the grass and drank freely of the water, using cupped hands to bring the cold water up to our mouths, quenching our thirst as the pure water flowed out of the earth. Crystal clear and cold, it emerged into the light for the first time, fresh, transparent and unpolluted. It flowed into a valley that had known only pollution for a number of decades, and it would be soon rendered undrinkable, but for the moment, we could enjoy its purity.

The sun was low in the sky. It would be dark in about two hours, and we needed to start back if we were to arrive home before it got too dark. We had about half an hour to spare; we could walk back in about two hours, and we were not worried if it was dark before we arrived home. Mog knew these mountains like the back of his hand, and could find his way home in total darkness. The water was cold, and Mog remarked, with a wicked look in his eyes, "I bet you sixpence you will not paddle in the stream for five minutes with your shoes and socks off."

"That is easy," I replied.

I accepted the challenge eagerly and the gamble was about to start. Bare foot, I stepped into the water, which went up to my ankles. Mog, watch in hand, counted the seconds. After a minute, I could feel the cold hitting my feet. I gritted my teeth and kept my feet firmly in the water, thinking of the sweets that could be bought with the money. The time seemed to last for ever but, eventually, he shouted, "Time's up. You win."

I pulled my feet out of the water, cold and a bit numb. He rubbed them for a few seconds, and the feeling started to return as I was putting my socks and shoes on.

"Where is the sixpence?" I chuckled, still feeling the chill in my feet. The money was handed over and we laughed, appreciating the feeling of being together and the enjoyment of each other's company. The walk back was slow; we were in no rush to arrive home, we were walking and talking as we moved forward. The day had been perfect; we had been walking from the early morning until the sun went down.

It was now dark and I was showing clear signs of tiredness. The moon was already out and bright. Mog was still full of life, as if he could go on without end. He had the strength of a bull, yet a determined gentleness that was like a jack in the box, you had to be alert or you would miss it as it jumped out at you, but it would be there if you knew him as I knew him.

"Hold on a minute! What is the rush?" he asked, placing his hand on my shoulder as if urging me to stop. "I feel like a few trout for breakfast, and your mother is partial to a bit of fresh fish as well."

The stars were now full out, twinkling high above our heads like hundreds of little dots. The full moon looked like a large crystal shimmering and glittering, throwing its night light onto the river, creating an eerie transparency as it penetrated into the water and reflected off its surface.

"How can we catch a trout in the dark? We need the light of day to fish-tickle," I replied in a tired voice, thinking that there is no way we will be able to catch fish, no matter how bright the moon and stars.

He just looked at me and smiled.

"Just you wait and see. You must outsmart the fish," he laughed.

He sat on the bank and from his pocket pulled out a piece of string and a mirror.

"Here, hold these for a minute," he said, handing me the two objects and delving back into his pocket. He pulled out a small torch. "Fetch me that long branch of wood and the two short sticks," he ordered, pointing to a few sticks near the riverbank. I did as asked and waited to see what he would do next.

With the string he tied the two short branches together in the form of a cross, placed the longer branch into the centre of the cross and tied it securely into the joints where the pieces of wood crossed over each other.

"Almost finished," he grunted, obviously satisfied with the results.

He tied the torch on to the end of the longest branch, removed his shoes and socks, and carried the whole construction into the water, resting the end of the longest branch on the bank, to act as an anchor and support. The two cross sections he placed into the water, standing them upright, with the torch on the end pointing down into the water.

"Steady the long branch on the bank," he shouted to me from the water."

"How do I do that?" I asked, now more confused than ever.

"Get a few large stones and place them over the end of the branch on the bank, to act as a weight; it will steady the other end."

I immediately obeyed and Mog remained up to his knees in the water, holding the cross sections of wood.

The task now complete, he came out of the water.

"What now?" I enquired.

He took the mirror, went back into the water and placed the glass on the gravel in the riverbed, directly under the torch, mirror side facing upward.

"Everything is ready. Stand back from the bank, and get ready to catch the fish when I throw them to you," he shouted, waving his hands to show me where he wished me to stand.

He turned on the torch and the light beam shone down into the water, directly over the mirror, which reflected the light back to the surface. Mog leaned over a large stone in the river, with his hand in the water near the mirror, and waited. A few minutes later, a fish swam over to the light, and I could see its tail moving slowly as it seemed to rest on the mirror, believing it was the moonlight. A quick flick of his hand and the fish flew out of the water and landed on the bank near to where I was standing; it was thrashing frantically in shock at its sudden unexpected exit from the moonlit water.

"Give it a tap on the head. Hurry up; don't let it suffer," Mog shouted.

I obeyed and, a moment later, the fish lay quiet. We had our first fish. This went on for a while, until we had caught five fish, two for my mother and three for Mog. He dismantled the wood, placed the torch and mirror back in his pocket, used the string to tie the fish together, and we were on our way again.

"How did you learn to do that?" I asked, totally intrigued.

If I had not seen it with my own eyes, there is no way I would have believed the manner in which the fish were caught.

"This technique was shown to me, when I was your age, by an old miner we referred to as John the Pit."

"Why was he called that?" I enquired, wondering what this had to do with the way these fish were caught.

"Because he was always catching fish and was never in the pit. If you saw him, you would know. He was built like an old pit pony, and had a back as strong as an ox. He would be over the river with his torch for hours at a time, when he should have been working. Come on, it is dark and you have asked enough questions. Let's get home."

We walked home, carrying the fish just caught. Twenty minutes later, we were in my house. My mother made us both food, and I was falling asleep over the meal.

"Go and wash your hands and face, and then, straight up to bed with you," she said, noticing that my eyes were closing.

"You have walked him off his feet, Mog" she added, looking intently at her brother with a grin on her face.

A few minutes later, I was in bed, leaving my mother and

Mog smoking cigarettes together. I hit the pillow and immediately fell asleep, happy and contented to think that I knew the source of the river, and forever grateful for my uncle Mog and his peculiar ways.

Chapter 11

S EVERAL SMALL STREAMS ran down both sides of the mountain, converging into the Fishing River, until the water found its level at the valley bottom, where the main river flowed. A lot of this water was siphoned off and used by the colliery to wash the coal, before its transportation to Cardiff to export abroad. The river always looked black and the river bed was covered with coal dust. There was another pit further down, called the Dare Colliery, and the water would be used here, too. When water reached Treorchy it was dirty and black and almost incapable of sustaining any fish life. A few specimens were able to survive in this murky substance but not many. Before the pits came, salmon travelled up this far, to spawn in the clear water.

As the water flowed past the pit, the whole of the river was arched over, from just before the pit started right through to the end. A number of smaller arches joined this main archway, bringing the water in by a series of small tunnels, all leading into the main tunnel. These smaller tunnels were just high enough to walk into, and a full grown adult had to bend his head. We were always told to keep out of these areas; they were extremely dangerous and dark. After heavy rain, the tunnels were full of water, and to fall into it, or be in the tunnel, at these times could be perilous.

To this warning we paid not the slightest attention. We knew where the tunnels started and knew where they came out, so, we thought, where is the danger? There were hazards everywhere, for those living near a colliery. We were used to living around danger. So where is the problem? We were not in the slightest worried. These tunnels were our play area; we saw no danger, only fun.

One Saturday morning, a few of us got together and decided to walk from one end of the tunnel to the other. The river was low and we wanted adventure. Deadeye Thomas was one of the gang, and he was now firmly established as the hot shot with the pellet gun. The cockerel incident must have concentrated his mind, and he would now at least see the target before shooting. There was a definite improvement in his hunting skills, in this respect. There were five of us for this journey into the underworld.

By eleven o'clock, we had collected candles, rope, wire and torches. The only other thing needed was a lunch packet, and that was easy to obtain. We smuggled out bread, cheese and a few biscuits from our houses. We were now ready to become moles for the next few hours. We knew, if our parents were to find out, there would be some explaining to get through, but we reasoned that this would be unlikely and this risk would be small.

One of us felt we should tie the rope around us, so we would all be together should one of us fall. The rest of us thought this of no value, except Kevin, who suggested, "Let's tie a rope at one end of the tunnel, and follow it through to the other, in case we get lost."

"How can we get lost, Kev? The tunnel starts one end and finishes the other. We can only go forward or backward," David asked, totally perplexed.

Kevin thought for a moment and then he smiled and said excitedly, "I've cracked it. If we follow the direction of the water, we cannot get lost; we are bound to come out at the other end."

Kevin had a knack of saying the obvious; the water flowed through the tunnel and so it must come out the other end. Gerald shook his head in disbelief and sarcastically commented, "What a good idea, Kev. All follow the water, boys."

The sarcasm was lost on Kev, and he felt satisfied that his idea was to be acted upon.

We decided to just stay close together as we walked into the tunnel. Deadeye went first, declaring boldly, "Follow me, boys," ever the optimist in the face of danger, followed by Gerald and the rest of us. Immediately the tunnel is entered you become aware of the darkness, the only natural light comes from the entrance. As you move further into the tunnel, the light becomes a dot in the distance, and then there is total darkness. The only light from this point on comes from the two torches we had with us and the few candles. The water was always low at this time of the year, but was still strong, and we needed to watch our footing.

In certain areas were large pools that the water had gouged out of the floor over the years, and the depth of water in some of these holes would have come over our heads. On more than one occasion, we lost our footing on the slippery floor of the tunnel and fell into the water. We were having fun, shouting laughing and generally making a noise, trying to frighten each other. We were all frightened by now, but none of us would ever admit it. We were on an adventure and would be brave in front of each other.

Onward we went, torches flashing around the tunnel and reflecting the light off the stalactites suspended from the ceiling, different shadows dancing all around us. We were peering into the darkness, and reading frightening thoughts into every new shadow.

There was constant noise in the tunnel: the sound of dripping water, and the whole tunnel seemed alive and frightening. We felt alone and isolated, only our sense of bravado kept us together. The darkness started to feel threatening; we could feel the claustrophobic surroundings slowly closing in. There were monsters and dark demons behind every shadow. We had been in the tunnel for over an hour and a half. The fun of the adventure was starting to turn cold on us. We were all wet, and the dampness seemed to stick to our clothes and was starting to affect us. We wanted our mothers and the other end of the tunnel, and we wanted them quickly.

Then, without warning, one of the torches went down on us.

"Keep shining the torch," Deadeye said, rather startled. The torch gave its last flicker of light and it went out. The batteries in the one remaining torch were starting to run down.

"The other torch is not very bright. Light a candle, and be quick about it," Gerald told Kevin, fear clearly showing in his voice.

"The wind in the tunnel keeps blowing out the light. I need help to shield the candle against this draught," Kevin responded. "Everything is damp, I don't like it any more," he added, in a faltering voice.

"Try, Kev," I remonstrated, just as the other torch was accidentally dropped into the water and all the light was gone. We were in trouble.

There was now total and utter darkness, no light was able to penetrate the tunnel, and we could not see a thing. Our eyes had become accustomed to the dark, but, in the total blackness, we just stood still for a moment and started to shout to each other for comfort.

"Light the candle. Hurry up," the cry went out.

A candle was eventually lit and shielded by cupped hands. Just as the candle was lit, there was one almighty splash. Kevin had fallen into the water and was in it up to his waist. He shouted loudly, his voice echoing in the damp tunnel.

"Get me out. I'm cold and wet. I've knocked my side."

None of us laughed; we were all frightened.

"Hold our hands, Kev," two of us shouted, and helped him out of the water, with just enough light from the candle, still carefully shielded by the other two.

Then, Brian fell into the water; the excitement of the moment combined with the slippery wet floor of the tunnel had made him lose his balance. We knew the tunnel must come to an end; we could not go back; the passageway could not last much longer, so forward we went, candle lit, candle out, candle lit, and candle out, according to how well it was shielded. Most of the time, there was total darkness and we were feeling our way along the sides of the wall. At last, we could see a faint light in the distance.

"I can see light, ahead, look! It won't be long now. Keep together," David said exultantly, shivering. We knew it could only be the daylight and the tunnel end. The light was a speck in the distance, but knowledge that the journey was about to end empowered us to keep going.

Twenty minutes later, we were in the sunlight, wet, cold, but happy. Deadeye was the first to speak.

"I was not frightened in the least. I jumped in the water deliberately, for a swim."

We all nodded in agreement and claimed that we were only pretending to be frightened. We were safe now, so no one wished to lose face with the rest of the group.

"Let's go back through the other way," Deadeye proposed, to show how brave he was, knowing full well this would never happen.

The sandwiches were wet and soggy, totally inedible, and had to be thrown away, but we had all completed the tunnel and this would be a story we would discuss for many months to come, and boast about how we were not afraid when we were in the dark. The reality of this foolish journey meant we were lucky to all be safe; things could have turned out very differently, but we were all a bit wiser, even if we did not admit the fact to each other. I slept soundly that night, warm and comfortable, safe in my own bed, happy that the shadows were no more than that, and now just memories.

There were numerous brothers in my father's family: Tommy, Idwal, Jim, and Jack, There had been a sister, but she died of scarlet fever when she was twenty-one years of age. This was still a tender area for him, and he said that his mother never really recovered after her death. Often, he would get up to start the day shift, before he was married, and his mother would be in the front room, crying for the loss of her only daughter. This brought the brothers closer together, and Tommy, being the eldest, was always held in the highest esteem.

Often, Tommy walked from Treorchy to our house; and my father and he would sit in the garden and talk, always in the Welsh language. Idwal was the youngest by two years and lived in Treherbert, and he also walked to Cwmparc to join the other two. Into this trio Jim, their cousin, would sometimes turn up, and when all four were together, they would end up in the Tremains Hotel, collecting Jim, the other brother, on the way, to ease the conversation with liquid refreshments.

The other brother, Jack, lived in London, but I did not know him at this time. My father said he was quite the ladies' man, tall, elegant and a bit of a dandy, always trimming his moustache in front of the mirror, before going on the town in Treorchy. He used to work in the pit, but moved to work in London when there were hard times in the colliery. There would always be a fondness in the voice of the brothers when they talked about Jack; he was the only one that left the valley, and they were proud that he took the chance to "Better Himself."

Arriving home from school one day, I found our house very quiet; this was unusual because there would always be something happening. There was always noise of one sort or another. My food was placed in front of me, and my parents moved into the front room to talk. This was extremely rare and I knew there must be something wrong.

After about ten minutes, my father came out of the front

room, tears in his eyes. This I had never seen before.

He said, "Jack has been in a car crash and is in Stoke Mandeville Hospital. It is expected he will not survive, and even if he does, he will be totally paralysed from the neck down."

I could feel the hurt in my father. I held out my hands and said, "Sorry, sorry. Daddy, don't be unhappy."

I ran over to him and held his leg. He did not say a word at first, just placed his hand on my head as if to gain comfort.

"We are all unhappy; this is a blow to us all," he said, and walked out of the house and into the garden. I was going to follow but my mother said, "No, your father needs to be alone. See him when he returns."

A lot more information came to light over the next few days. All the brothers met to assess the situation, the bond that was forged many years earlier between them, when their parents were alive, was now closer than ever. The hurt was real; they were feeling the pain of their own kin. Jack was their brother, and his life was in the balance. The ring of self-assurance between them, that was rounded and unbroken to date, was now under threat. There was a wholesome and unconditional commitment given to each other years earlier, and now one of the brothers needed help. They would need to be united. Trouble with a big T had arrived, but what could they do?

The first and most obvious thing was to pay a visit and to assess the full extent of Jack's injuries. He had a wife and son and they were in regular contact, but there is nothing like direct action, if only to make them feel they were doing something.

Preparations were undertaken for the trip to Aylesbury. My father had never been out of Wales, so a trip to the hospital would be quite an ordeal. I could see the stress in his face. He did not like travelling far, and to travel all that way at such short notice made him feel nervous. The following day, the brothers were on their way.

They returned a few days later, downcast and sad. They had seen their brother Jack, lying on his back, unable to move a single muscle, paralysed from the neck down. This sight physically upset all the brothers; there was nothing any of them could do to help. The car Jack was travelling in had collided with another car on the motorway, and his spine was broken just below the neck.

They got some satisfaction from the hospital's statement that they would start therapy in a few weeks and there could be some improvement. My father believed Jack would walk again, and clung to this belief more out of hope and blind faith than from reason or common sense. We are all the same when we do not wish to face an unpalatable and obvious fact: we interpret the situation according to our beliefs and will not face the inevitable until we are forced to. My father was unable to accept; he was in denial of the facts, and no amount of reality would change his mind.

"Jack will walk again, you wait and see. The doctors are not always right," he stubbornly insisted to my mother, who was more of a realist. She knew what the true situation was, but this was not the right time to make my father confront reality.

Jack was the main topic of conversation in our house, and the reports we were getting from the hospital about the therapy were not encouraging. There was no movement in his legs or arms; his whole body was limp. He could only move his eyes. If he needed a cigarette, someone had to place one in his mouth and take it out for him after each drag. It was now nearly a month since the accident, and Jack was still the same. My father still could not accept the fact that he would not walk again. Everyone else knew the truth of it, but no one dared to state the obvious in front of my father.

Chapter 12

THE TIME OF YEAR was coming for the Sunday school annual outing. Once a year, on a Saturday, there was a trip by train to Barry Island, paid for by the Church. We all used to look forward to this trip from Treorchy to the island. The night before, my mother would be preparing everything: sandwiches, crisps, chocolate bars and bottles of lemonade. The more we took with us, the less we needed to purchase, so the cheaper the day would turn out. There would be extra clothes, towels, sun lotions, and a whole host of other things packed, to help us to enjoy the day.

We would all catch the bus from Cwmparc to Treorchy and travel on the 9 o'clock train. The journey to Barry took about an hour and twenty minutes. The train started fifteen minutes earlier, at Treherbert, and came into the station at Treorchy, showing a full head of steam. The old steam trains were a sight we all liked, chugging noisily along the track, steam rising high in the air, with the smell of grease, oil, and coal burning. The excitement was electric as we waited to board the train; the platform would be full, everyone talking at the same time, and no one really listening, but all excited about the trip and happy for the day about to start. The train stopped, the carriage doors opened, the rush, the children moved through the train, looking where to sit, baskets and bags seemed everywhere, as well as the crowd. Disorganisation seemed to be the order of the day, and yet there still prevailed a strange kind of consideration for other people.

Doors closed, the whistle blew, we were off, all the children looking out of the windows, shouting to one another, parents shouting at them to close the windows, children taking not the slightest bit of notice, parents shuffling into their seats, children already eating sweets or chocolate; hustle and bustle everywhere, the journey to Barry Island was under way. The sound of a steam engine moving along the track; you inside the carriage, on an outing to Barry Island, was unforgettable.

The train stopped at a few stations as it progressed down the valley and then, it steamed straight to Barry. The station there was opposite the fairground and, as the train moved into the station, all windows were full of children anxious to see who could catch sight of the sea first. The first signs of water would see the whole carriage, children and parents alike, explode in excitement as the sea was approached.

"I see it. I saw the sea first," one of the children shouted.

"No, you didn't. I saw the water before you," another replied, with the first one taking not the slightest of notice.

The fairground was in full view. Parents were trying in vain to keep a grip on the children. The whole trainload was happy and excited; we had arrived.

At the island, we would look for a pitch, a kind of base camp. We would hire deck chairs and place them in a circle, bags would be placed under the chairs, and all the children would be called together by the adults. We were told to mark where we were all seated, and various landmarks were pointed out, in case we got lost. The buckets and spades were placed in the centre of the ring of deck chairs, for the children to play with in the sand, allowing the parents to settle down into the chairs and quickly fall asleep, the children around their feet, throwing sand and making noises.

The men would place hankies on their heads, to protect themselves from the sun. The women would wear headscarves or hats; the latter in all types of colours and shapes, and looked out of the ordinary and funny, to any passer by, but to our party they seemed natural and right. It gave the group a kind of cohesion, when away from home.

The children dug in the sand and made castles with their buckets, the men helping in this task from time to time, more to show the women folk they were lending a hand with the children than out of enjoyment. Drinks, ice cream or ice lollies would be dispensed, and food would be available throughout the day, in an atmosphere of sharing and caring for each other.

As lunch time approached, there was a feeling of expectancy among the men, who would look round, point at objects of interest around the beach that they would like to see, the eyes moving from one corner of the beach to the other, trying to attract the attention of the other men, without the women noticing. They were starting to sweat and get thirsty; they needed a walk. Playing with the kids and sleeping on the deck chairs was taking its toll. They needed a break and would all be actively looking for any excuse to leave the circle and manoeuvre themselves to the nearest drinking hole. They had already promised the women that they would stay on the beach all day, but making a promise and keeping it against these pressures seemed more than human nature is able to bear. They wanted release from this promise given in bed, at a time when a man would agree to anything, when he wanted the woman's favours.

The excuses would follow one after another.

"I need to stretch my legs," one of them would state, standing up and stretching as if to demonstrate how stiff his legs were. This would be quickly followed by another comment.

"Where are the toilets?" Every person in the party was fully aware of the whereabouts of the toilets. The women were used to this behaviour and put up only token resistance to the men wishing to leave the group and go walkabout, not holding them to past promises. The pubs were open and the men were thirsty. One by one, at a few minutes interval, so as not to attract the attention of the vicar and churchwardens in another circle, they would all wander away, leaving the women and children talking and playing in the circle.

The pub would be full to capacity, most of the men on the trip ended up there at some time in the afternoon, smiling and happy to be drinking; contented to stare into the frothy liquid in the glass for a large part of the afternoon, and in high spirits as their wives looked after the children. The men needed to be away from the women and children for a few hours. It was their way of being masculine in a mainly male-dominated society. They were used to working with their male colleagues and felt at ease when they were all together, drinking and telling stories, generally about nothing important. It was a way of releasing tension and taking their minds off the hardness, harshness and ruggedness of their existence. For a lot of them, this would be the only holiday they would get. Some of the lucky ones might have a caravan holiday in Porthcawl, during miners' fortnight, if they were fortunate, but that would be their lot. Today, they would enjoy themselves and be happy, forget about the way they live, and let tomorrow look after tomorrow.

We paddled in the sea, splashing and throwing seaweed all over one another; dug holes on the sand, only to have the waves wash over them and render them flat. Sand would be everywhere: in our hair, on our hands and bodies, but this was all part of the fun.

We ran into the waves and washed the sand off, only to come out of the water and be back in the same predicament. A favourite game was to pop the seaweed and listen to the sound made as we squeezed out any air trapped in the cavities. The long strands we placed around our necks and ran around pretending to be pit horses. All would have a good time and, every time we came back from the water, there were crisps, lemonade, and chocolate for us as we dried ourselves.

As the afternoon progressed, all the children started to get excited. The highlight of the day was nearing; the time when we were to visit the fairground. All food and drink would be consumed by the late afternoon, the litterbins overflowing with the day's waste. The bags would be much lighter now and, after the deck chairs were taken back and our deposits refunded, we were ready to move into the fair. This was always about two hours before the train arrived to take us home. The fair was an expensive place, and you could see the money being counted by the women, in order to measure how many rides they were able to afford for us to go on.

A trip to the fair would not be complete unless we had candy floss, rolled and made in front of our eyes. The stick went round and round, the candy ball growing ever larger. The sticky pink candy would be everywhere, all over our mouths, faces, and hands. The taste was sugary and sweet as we sucked the floss into nothing.

"Can I go on the ghost trains, mammy?" I would shout excitedly. "They really are my favourite."

We would all go on together; my middle brother shouting and screaming the loudest as the train moved around all the scary creatures in the tunnel.

"Hold my hands," I shouted to my mother in the seat opposite, laughing and frightened all at the same time, in a frenzy of heightened awareness. "Look out, that monster is going to swallow us," I screamed at the top of my voice as the train entered the mouth of a large demon belching smoke. There would be a fright around every turn, and laughter and shouts could be heard all through the tunnel as the train proceeded round the track.

There was the big wheel ride, the slow train rides, water chute slide, the distorted mirror tunnel, the shaking bridge, and many more. The men went on the dodgems with their children, the women looking on with delight, waving and laughing. The cars travelled round and round, crashing into each other as they bounced forward and backwards.

We all left the fair, happy and laughing. The men were always looking for the toilet, to give back most of the liquid consumed in the afternoon, but the moment would be perfect, and we would all be excited and full of energy as we went to catch the train home to our Valley.

The journey home would be one of laughter and merriment as we recalled the day to each other.

"Did you go round and round on the wheel?" one child would enquire.

Another would exclaim, "The mirror made me look six feet tall and as fat as an elephant." A third would show the passengers the goldfish he had won, boasting, "I had to throw all the rings over the peg, to win."

Everyone would be talking about what they got up to on the sand, in the sea, and at the fair. Several people would be talking at once, more interested in telling their story than in listening to what someone else had to say. A few would have caught too much sun and would be red all over, only to be told that they should have been more careful, while being shown little sympathy.

The train arrived at Treorchy station and we all piled out onto the platform and watched the train move away up the valley to Treherbert, its final destination. The women gathered the children together, now tired and exhausted, and headed for the bus stop, too tired to walk up to Cwmparc.

"Any one for a pint of beer, to round off the day?"

A few of the men headed across the road to the Pengelli Hotel, to finish off the day, contented to think that they had done their duty.

Chapter 13

THE SUMMER WAS MOVING forward and all the hard work in the garden was showing results; the carrots, potatoes, cabbages, runner beans, as well as the other vegetables, were in full growth and ready to be picked and eaten fresh. The runner beans were a special favourite, picked when tender, cut into lengths and boiled, then served on a plate with butter and eaten with fresh bread; what a taste! The hard work in the garden was over for the year, with the rewards to look forward to. A lot of the vegetables my father gave away, contented with the knowledge that he grew them, and wishing to share as much as possible of the produce of his garden with the neighbours.

The time I spent in the garden at this time of the year was long; on some days, I was there from early in the morning until the sun went down. These days will forever remain fresh and alive in my mind, and had a profound influence on my character for the rest of my life. Many times, my father and I would be in the field, cutting back the rushes with a sickle. A part of the field was bog and, in the dry weather, we hacked at these rushes and spread them on the grass to dry out. When dry, we would place them in bags and store them in the cowshed to use for winter bedding for the cattle. This was backbreaking work. You were either on your knees, or bent over, with your back arched, as you wielded the sickle. The sweat streamed down our faces and there would be blisters on the palm of my hand, due to the friction created by the handle of the sickle. When I stopped work, the skin on the palm of my hand would be rubbed raw, and it bled as the blisters burst.

"Here, rub your hands with a few dock leaves," my father

would say, handing me a handful he had just pulled from the ground. "Squeeze them into the blisters and let the juice from the leaf fall into the cuts."

I did as told and felt the pain coursing through my hand as the leaf's juices ran over the skin. The smarting would be intense at first but, after a while, the pain would lessen, giving way to relief. I would tie a rag around my hand and carry on working, not dreaming of giving up until the job was complete. As time went on, and with constant exposure to this work, the hands toughened and I developed hard calluses that allowed me to handle the tool without the skin breaking.

My father was troubled all the time and had not been his usual self since Jack had the accident. As each day passed, he became more withdrawn, and I knew he was worried about the situation. He had been to see Jack a few times over recent months, and was always depressed when he returned. One time, when we were both resting in the field, we sat on the grass and started to drink from the bottle of water we always had with us. He lit his pipe, looked at me and said, "Family, boy, is one of the most important things in life. They are part of us, our own flesh and blood, and when in troubled waters, we must support each other. Always remember this with your brothers, because I will not always be around to help."

I thought at first he was going to talk about our family and my two younger brothers, but he was referring to himself and his brothers.

We did not speak for a few moments, and I asked, "Will Uncle Jack ever walk again?"

I received no answer, and asked the question again.

"Do you think Uncle Jack will be able to walk, when he gets better?"

This time, my father looked straight into my eyes and spoke slowly.

"He will walk again. The legs need constant attention but,

with the right exercise and medical treatment, there is no doubt he will be able to walk. Look at Jim up the road; he is walking again."

These words were spoken with total conviction; there was obviously no doubt in my father's mind that Jack would walk again, and he was hatching a plot to bring this about.

We carried on cutting the rushes. I stopped for a while, to watch my father; each cut was perfect and precise, as the sickle was wielded. He was cutting the reeds in one constant movement, with a swish and whoosh, as the implement cut through the air. He was troubled and was trying to divert his thoughts by hard work, but as yet, he could not find an answer.

That weekend, I awoke to the sound of banging in the room below the bedroom. My father, hammer in hand, was moving the partition between the passage way and our front parlour. The parlour was small, with only enough room for a few pieces of furniture, which we were just about able to walk between. This was our best room and used only on special occasions and on Christmas Day, and he was knocking the partition down and opening up the whole room. My mother did not seem to mind, which was unusual. I thought for a minute that they had both gone mad and would start knocking down the whole house. They seemed happy and contented, with my father singing his favourite song.

As I walked past the pair of them, my mother, hair all over her face, told me, "Get your own breakfast. We are all too busy. There is plenty to eat in the cupboard."

"What is going on? Why are you knocking the house down?" I enquired, rather alarmed.

"Never you mind. Just go and help yourself to breakfast," my mother responded. "Afterwards, you can help to move the remains from the dismantled partition," she added.

My father was singing at the top of his voice, my mother humming along to my father's words. The whole area was in a mess, there was dust everywhere, piles of rubbish all over the passage and floor of what was shortly to become one room. If I had not seen this sight, I would never have believed this was happening. I looked at Gwyn, my middle brother, and we both shrugged our shoulders in amazement.

This was the happiest I had seen my father since his brother's accident, and there was contentment about the house that morning. Happiness is contagious, it spreads like light entering the window in the early morning, and it was spreading now. It made us feel happy, yet slightly mad with the whole situation. The problem that had inflicted a melancholy halo over my father was gone, lifted, blown away, moved on; our house was happy but dusty and full of rubbish. Dust and dirt did not matter to us, the spirit of optimism was in the air, and we were all caught up in it, the mood was good, the house was happy.

I ate my breakfast and went back into the other room.

"What do you want me to do?" I asked, waiting to be told exactly what was happening. My parents smiled and before my father had time to explain, my mother replied, "Your uncle Jack is coming to live with us, and this is to be his room. The front room is too small, so the passage wall is coming down, to create extra space."

From our front door, you could walk straight up the stairs and into the two small bedrooms at the top. To the right of the front door we went straight into our passage. This was the partition being knocked down, and another door would be placed to the right of the front door, to stop the draught from directly entering the front room that was now one room. We would need to walk through this room to get to the back of the house, and, to protect Jack's privacy, a curtain would hang the full length of the room, left open most of the time, but it could be pulled together when a need for privacy arose.

My father was trained in First Aid and used to be called if any person needed help underground. He prided himself on this knowledge. He was convinced that, with regular exercise and continued support, his brother would walk again, and this support would be given by him. At last, he felt he was doing something positive and not standing on the side, hoping for the situation to right itself. Mog turned up, hammer under arm, ready to give a hand, and within a few days, the transformation of the room was complete, even down to the new wallpaper. A new bed was purchased by my father, together with a mattress designed especially for disabled people who spend a large proportion of their time in bed.

Arrangements were made for both my parents to go to fetch Jack from the hospital. They were to travel up by train and Jack's son, Donald, agreed to drive them all back in his car, after full consultation with the doctor.

When they were due back in the Valley, a message was sent, to say they were on the road. There would be many stops on the way back, and the journey would take all day. Another message arrived, stating they were about three to four hours away and would be with us at about six in the evening. We were looked after by Mair and Glyn, now firm friends of the family and ever ready to give a helping hand.

The last part of the journey took them over the Rhigos Mountain; this in response to a request from Jack, who wished to stop on the top of the mountain and look down over the Valley.

"This is a sight I never thought to see again. What a sight! I love this Valley, for all its problems," he exclaimed, picking out the different landmarks. He was coming home to the land of his parents, and these thoughts and feelings were welling up inside him. He was paralysed from the neck down, unable to move, but still feeling the emotions of being human and the pull of the Valley; remembering the warmth of home and his childhood. He knew these mountains, the streams, the coal tips, and he was feeling the pull deeply, as it was tearing at his heart.

These tears of happiness, after what he had been through, were rolling down his face. Unable to wipe his own eyes without help, this task was performed by his brother. The tears were not only in Jack's eyes, but also in my parents'; the sensation was shared; all eyes were wet as they looked at Jack. Donald, his son, could not speak because of the emotion of the moment, and expressed himself by just looking at his father with total happiness, his glad heart glowing with warmth because his father was happy and home.

They arrived at six thirty on a Monday afternoon. The car pulled up outside our house, my father and Jack were in the back, my mother and Donald in the front. The trauma of seeing my uncle, a person who could not move a muscle, produced revulsion and sudden shock in my mind. I had never seen a paralysed person before. My father seemed to not notice how I felt. He was preoccupied with getting Jack into the house and settled into bed.

"Say hello to your uncle," my father remarked happily.

"Hello," I said, in a disgusted tone, and walked away.

I knew about death and my first thought was that this man should be dead. He could not move, not even to go to the toilet. My heart went out to this uncle, yet a feeling of sadness seemed to overwhelm me that any human being could be allowed to suffer this much. Why my uncle? Life is not fair. These were the thoughts in my head. I felt ashamed for the way I was feeling. I could not even look at him for long; it turned my stomach; and yet I did not know how to control my attitude to the situation. His life was over, why is he not dead?

This thought would not go away. I knew it was wrong but could do nothing. I thought of other things, but I kept wishing, with all the power of a storm crashing and lashing into me, that this man was dead. Why did we bring him home? A tree had more movement in its branches than my uncle had in his limbs.

I wanted to cry and feel happy for my father, all at the same time. A feeling of cold hatred surged through my veins. I hated myself for these thoughts. Why was I not feeling that total happiness everyone else seems to be enjoying? I was isolated and felt alone, lost in my beliefs, mixed, confused, sad, and ashamed, all in the same instant.

My father carried Jack into the house. He looked frail but happy as he was placed on the bed, to rest and to recuperate after the long journey. There was a sense of achievement in the house. Jack was home, opposite was the house where he was born, below that was the colliery where he had worked, the garden his father had tended was around the corner. The whole place was familiar. He was where he thought he would never be again: in his home. Everyone knew him and this made me feel ashamed for my earlier thoughts. Why was I the only one to feel this way? Could it be that we all had the same feelings but were unable to admit to them, even to ourselves? If one of my father's animals were suffering like this, I knew what the outcome would be, and it would be immediate; but this is human life, and different rules must apply.

The following day, after Jack had enjoyed a solid sleep, the neighbours started to arrive. Jack was sitting up in bed. My father had already prepared him for the day to come. His body needed massaging and moving constantly, as well as all the toiletry functions, the usual washing and cleaning of the body, that needed to be completed every morning and several times throughout the day; all these were to become routine. It was necessary to avoid bed sores and try to prevent the skin from rubbing into the bedclothes. Jack needed to be turned every hour or two, to avoid constant pressure on the same spot, and my father was going to do all in his power to see that everything possible that could be done would be done.

The first to arrive was Jim from up the street, who knew all about disability from the time when he broke his back in the colliery, several years ago. His recovery had been remarkable. He came through the door, bent double, stick in hand, pipe in mouth, and smiling.

"Well, Jack, you are in a bit of a mess, old boy."

"You could say that, Jim. I have no movement in my whole body." Jack was smiling, happy to see his cousin.

Jim sat by his side and held his hand. Jack looked down and said, "Sorry, I cannot feel your hand. Could you place it on my head. I am able to feel your hand there."

Jim placed his hand on Jack's head without question, and you could see and feel the warmth in this gesture. Two old friends since childhood were meeting for the first time after a few years, both paralysed, one worse than the other, Jim because of Black Gold, the other because he tried to get away from it and ended up in a car crash.

"Light me a cigarette, could you, Jim?" Jack asked.

Jim lit the cigarette and held it to Jack's mouth, in order for him to take a drag. He removed the cigarette after each drag, to allow Jack to exhale the smoke through his mouth.

"Remember when I was in hospital after my accident, and you held a cigarette for me, Jack, hiding it from the nurses?"

They both laughed.

"That nurse sure was a good looker, do you recall, Jim?"

"A ladies' man to the end, hey, Jack?"

There was more laughter.

"I remember. How could I forget that you asked her out on a date?" he added, smiling. They carried on reminiscing about old times and the fun they shared as children and how the rolls were now reversed.

"Life is a funny taskmaster. None of us knows the future, but at least you are home," Jim said, as he touched Jack's head again.

The next to arrive, about twenty minutes later, was Jack's

brother Jim from across the road. Jim had seen Jack arrive last evening, but this was the first time they had time to speak together.

"How are you feeling today, after that long journey?"

"Well, I do not feel, if that is what you mean. The only things I am able to move are my eyelids, and they feel in tip top condition this morning," was the reply.

They all laughed at this, as Jim, his brother, spoke.

"See, Jack, you have the advantage over us. You always were a dandy one and the sharpest of the brothers."

More laughter and banter and point scoring, as if they were underground, working together, my father listening to the chat in the other room, and feeling a warm glow inside. After all he had been through, Jack could still laugh, and laughter is the greatest tonic in life.

The room was full of smoke, but they were used to this and did not seem to notice the smell or the atmosphere in the room. Towards mid day, Idwal turned up, and, later, Tommy; all the brothers were now together, laughing and smiling, telling each other funny stories and anecdotes, the bond was as strong as ever. The room was full and time seemed to be unimportant as the day progressed. Jack was turned every hour, and at lunchtime, he was placed in his wheelchair for a while, before he was to settle back into bed for his afternoon rest.

Jack had the worst type of paralysis. The only movement was in his neck and head. All toiletry functions were gone and he needed constant attention, and help to eat, to smoke, to wipe his nose, even. On some occasions, his legs would shake in spasms, but this was not due to any feeling, it was because the leg muscles were wasting and the nerves were shocked into a sudden movement. His hands would also shake, and when this happened often, my father would hold his hand gently, to minimise the affect of the nervous spasm.

Our front parlour was small, with a tiny grate in the centre of the wall dividing ours from the next terraced house. A bed was in the corner opposite the window, a small chair was next to the bed, with a larger chair under the window. This was all the available space could hold. If there were more guests, a few small chairs could be brought into the room, and the room was full. The curtain could be pulled right across the room, and was used to create privacy. In one corner was a wooden box that could act as a seat and it held all the items needed for the care of the invalid. There were cotton wool, bandages, and ointment for bedsores, bottles of all descriptions as well as all the toiletry paraphernalia. The box was full to the top, and often the contents would need to be squashed down, in order to close the lid.

That night, Jack was exhausted. The whole day had seen people calling, and the room was always full of people. Laughter was everywhere, it seemed to penetrate the whole house and even the smoky, heavy atmosphere took second place to this happiness. Jack sat propped up in bed with pillows all around him, cigarette in mouth, and one of the party moving the addictive weed continually as he inhaled. The damage had already been done to this proud body, so the smoke could do no further damage. He was enjoying the ambiance of the moment, and no person could deny him this, after what he had been through. It was good to see these friends and relatives sharing old memories and making new ones in a Valley that knew what hardship and companionship meant. The conversation was continuous, except when Jack needed changing and his medication.

"All out," my father would order. The room was then emptied, the curtain drawn, and the party would wait at the front door for the task to be completed. Mog or Jim, his cousin, would also help, and the three of them would often be behind the curtain while the rest waited. The waste would be disposed of; air freshener sprayed all around the room, and the conversation would start all over again, together with the constant cigarette smoking.

One day was like another day, one merging into the next. Routine is important when various repetitive tasks are to be performed, and my father had his schedule down to a fine art. Every morning before work, when he was on the day shift, he would be with Jack for at least half an hour, moving and massaging his legs, arms, feet, back and neck, trying desperately to find some form of movement in this bent and crippled body. Often, I could hear my father pulling and moving the body of his brother, and trying to convince himself that there was movement in his limbs. The same process would be conducted every evening, and my father was still convinced that his brother would walk again. He believed with all the conviction of a Christian that one day he would see Jack walk.

My mother gave total backing to my father, and sometimes ventured to discuss with him the false hope he held about his brother, but she could not broach the subject in a way that would make him listen. Everyone else knew that Jack was deteriorating, and the doctors gave him only a year, or at the most two, to live. His body was breaking down, he was in constant pain, he could often be heard moaning in distress, and he needed regular painkillers to relieve the agony. Oh, I wished to see him quiet and resting, even dead, and yet, hating myself for thinking this way, when my father had so much faith. What was wrong with me? I would often ask myself, am I really a bad person to believe this way?

A few days later, I was in the garden with my father. He could see there was something troubling me.

"What is wrong with you?" he asked.

"Nothing," I replied, in a dejected tone of voice, my eyes firmly looking down at the floor. My father did not immediately pursue this, but left the matter alone. We both worked in the garden and did not speak for a while, and then I asked, "Why is

Uncle Jack still alive?"

I said these words without thinking, and I thought my father would be annoyed. "Sorry, I did not mean to say these words. He is my uncle and I should love him," I said, trying to back track.

"Say what you mean. You are young and have your own thoughts. Do not be ashamed of your feelings," my father answered gently.

My thoughts started to race. How could my father be so calm, knowing that I wished his brother dead? He looked at me and smiled, lit his pipe and said, "Let's sit on the bench and discuss your thoughts a bit closer. Thoughts are funny things, and we are often unable to control what we feel. You have a right to how you feel, and I am glad you were able to share these feelings with me. They are not wrong. You have a right to feel and to think in a free fashion. This right is central to us being human. Do not deny your feelings, my boy, because, to suppress these thoughts will make you less than human."

I was now totally confused and could not grasp what I was being told. I had just told my father that I wish his brother were dead, and he told me I have a right to feel this way. He always taught me that life was precious and must be preserved at all costs, and now he is saying my thoughts are all right, and I have a right to feel this way. I stared for a moment at my father, and could not say a word. He just looked at me and waited for me to speak.

"My feelings are bad. Why can't I feel differently? Everyone else feels different about the situation. Why do I feel this way? I think uncle Jack should not be alive. I feel his life is over. Why does he live?"

My father puffed his pipe, pulled his hair down over his brow. He was wearing a large grin on his face, showing all his teeth. His hand moved slowly towards my head, touched my hair, and then he spoke.

"Where there is life there is hope. I hope that, one day, Jack might be a lot different. You are only looking at the shell. You are too young to have seen the inside. I have seen the pearl, and, in my eyes, it is perfect and beautiful. I look at Jack with the trained eye of the pearl fisherman and know what there is inside. I do not see a shell, unable to move and in constant pain."

He stopped speaking to relight his pipe, striking a match on a nearby stone, and continued.

"I remember the walks we went on, the way he would lift me up onto his shoulders, when I was a small boy, and take me for a walk, just like your uncle Mog. I think about the way he protected me from the bullies, and how he shared with me his last bit of food. I see a person alive and happy, not the shell that this accident has brought upon him, through no fault of his own. Do not judge by the cover; look inside the book, see through the haze and look to the beauty it hides."

I stared hard at the floor, thought for a few seconds, and answered, "I will try, daddy. I will look past the shell." I was determined to try to see the pearl my father had described in my uncle.

Chapter 14

THE NEXT DAY was a Saturday and I determined to spend most of the day with my uncle, to see if I, too, could find the pearl my father told me to look for, and to lift the fog from my eyes and see the beauty that lies beneath.

"Good morning, Uncle Jack. How are you this morning?"

"So and so, and up and down. Things are not too bad."

"Did you sleep well, Uncle Jack?"

"As well as can be expected. I woke up a few times in the night but, generally, it was so and so."

I sat by the side of the bed, looking at my uncle, but could not find anything positive to say. He moved his neck to look at me and asked, "How was school last week? Did you learn anything interesting?"

"No, school and me do not get on."

"Not get on! What do you mean?"

"I do not like school and school does not like me, so we do not get along together."

"Funny you should feel this way, because school and myself were never the best of friends. We were always quarrelling, and I could not wait to grow up and work down the pit and be a man," was his response, as he looked at me from his bed.

"I would like to work in the pit, but my father will not let me. He wants me to work in a factory, or on the land," I explained, feeling my uncle could be on my side.

"He has a point, you know. If we were all meant to work and live down a hole, we would have claws and a pointy nose, like a mole, and then we would all enjoy living down a hole."

This made me laugh out loud, as I looked at my uncle, who

was also laughing, moving his head from side to side, a wide smile on his face.

"What is it like down the pit, Uncle Jack? Is it very dark?"

The darkness of the tunnel was still clearly in the forefront of my mind, and the sensation of feeling alone and forgotten in an alien environment sent a cold shiver up my spine.

"The pit is dark and dangerous, and has ruined many a life, and will carry on ruining many more, so you cannot blame your father for feeling the way he does."

This made me think for a minute of the danger, and of how my grandfather had suffered. I knew he was right in what he said, but felt the pit was the destiny of all my family, and it would eventually be mine, in spite of my father's wishes. My uncle broke the tradition, to go to London, and this is the price he is now paying.

The next question astonished me; my uncle knew what I was thinking, and he said, "I left the pit for the bright lights of London, and look where it has got me. You must think that I should have stayed in the pit, and this would not have happened to me."

This is precisely what I was thinking, and my face went bright red and I could not speak for a moment. My uncle looked at me and added gently, "My life is all but over. Many people believe I would be better off dead, including me. I am lucky, though. Things could have been worse. This accident could have happened to me when I was a young man, like my cousin Jim." He stopped speaking for a moment and then continued. "We are becoming good friends, and that makes me feel lucky, so things are not all bad."

I thought, how could he say he was lucky? He was unable to move, totally dependent on other people, and he states that things could have been worse.

"Besides, I was in the car with Donald. It could have been him who was paralysed and not me. I am glad it was me and not my son. That makes me lucky."

These words startled me a bit. Young as I was, I started to look at the person and not the infirmity.

The words came out of my mouth before I realised what I was saying.

"Do not wish yourself dead, Uncle. We love you."

Why did I say these words? I did not mean them. Only a short while ago, I was discussing this very topic with my father, and saying how I wished my uncle dead. Jack stared deeply into my eyes, and I know that he knew what I was thinking, and I could not hold the contact with his eyes any longer. I could not stop my thoughts; all these feeling of inadequacy and shame came flooding back into my mind, my body felt as if I had touched an electric socket, and I was stung hard. My body shook with shame, and the more I tried to control these feelings, the less restraint I was able to exercise.

"Don't be afraid of your feelings. You are young and have a right to feel as you do. I feel the same way, and it is my life. I do not wish to live like this, but it is God's will, and who am I to challenge this great power? I do not have long left on this earth. I have had a good life, and my one wish is now fulfilled, thanks to your father."

He does not wish to live, I thought, and yet he feels lucky to be lying there instead of his son, I was starting to understand what my father had been saying.

"I never thought I would see the Valley again and the garden that your grandfather tended and now your father looks after."

"Are the family trees friends?" I enquired.

"Yes, good friends I never thought to see again. Their power extends beyond their leaves, and when I saw the hedge again, standing where it always stood, proud, upright and well groomed by your father, that made me feel lucky. The trees seemed to smile at me, as you would at an old friend," he agreed, moving his head from side to side. "I could feel the warmth in the leaves and the whispering as the wind moved through the branches, speaking only to me; saying, *Jack, you are home. Jack, you are home. It is good to see you again, old friend."*

He asked me to wipe his mouth with his handkerchief, which was on the end of the bed, and then, he continued.

"To see the Fishing River and to hear the water moving over the stones has been my dream since the accident happened, and to go down the Tremains Hotel and have a pint of beer with my childhood friends, to laugh, to tell old stories, to look back to how we were. These are important to me now. Look after your father. He is a treasure and a true friend, as well as a fine brother to me. It is he who made this happen. He is a good man, and his son can be no less of a person. Do not feel ashamed of your thoughts. They are honest and pure, and you cannot run away from your thoughts, because, wherever you are, they are there with you."

These words were spoken by a person who could not move, who was still proud in character but broken in body, and they made me feel proud of my family and my upbringing. My uncle was telling me of his hopes and dreams since the accident, and how my father made these very modest wishes possible. My thoughts were not different from my uncle's. He did not wish to live in his present form, but it's God's will, and he was telling me that what *will be, must be,* and my thoughts are no different from his own.

The more time I spent with my uncle, the less noticeable his disability seemed. The more I got to know him, the more my feelings changed. We talked, got to know each other as friends, sharing stories and my future dreams and aspirations. He shared with me his thoughts and imaginings when he was young, and what he wished for when wishes were something to believe in; how he went underground when he was only fourteen years of age. He spoke of the way the miners worked together, sharing their experiences, their troubles, their joys and dangers; they were one unit, united in their hardships and by shared experiences. These values I could identify with, the Valley people were brought up in the way of the miner, and the close community spirit was associated with Black Gold.

The weeks were moving forward. Every morning and evening, my father massaged Jack's legs and arms, moving them in the directions of the joints, to keep them supple for when he would walk again. This task was given priority and conducted with a dedication bordering on the fanatical. His muscles must not be allowed to waste, and continual massaging of the arms and legs would not allow this to happen. This massage would last for at least twenty minutes, and often a full half hour, every session.

Everyone except my father could see there was not the slightest improvement in Jack, but he clung to the slightest change and convinced himself there was movement in his brother's body. Even I knew my father was clutching at straws, but when a straw is all there is, you will grasp it. My father believed totally that he would see his brother walk again, even if the rest of us, including Jack, knew all hope had gone. My father's mind was strong and resolute, and his blind faith propelled him forward past the line of reason. He could not and would not accept what the rest of us knew.

Caring for his brother was taking its toll on my father, and often Glyn would do the nightly massages, or Mog. Davy, being a frequent visitor, helped whenever asked and sometimes took control, to give their friend Dai a rest, not because they thought it would do any good. Jack was deteriorating and there was nothing any of us on this earth could do about it. Jack's struggle to stay in this world was becoming increasingly difficult. The constant pain in his muscles, as they were failing, left everyone in no doubt that things were not improving, but moving towards another conclusion, a termination that was not yet accepted by my father.

Chapter 15

THE MORNINGS WERE GETTING colder and winter was just around the corner, frost was already starting to cover the ground at daybreak. Fires were piled high with coal, constantly raked and poked for maximum heat. This commodity was in plentiful supply and helped to keep many an old person alive through the cold nights of winter.

We were well into autumn; the wind was blowing down the valley, informing us that winter was to follow closely behind. The clouds were low in the sky, the sun hidden high in the heavens and not allowed to warm the earth below. Rain was the order of the day, rain which lasted all day and every day. The blanket of winter was encroaching; there was a chill in the air you could feel as you left the house.

This is the time of the year when the beauty of the summer hides, until it is woken by the gentle warmth of the sun in the spring. Trees lose their leaves, grass stops growing, birds fly south, the field mice and hedgehogs go into hibernation for the winter. As one beauty fades, another moves to replace it. Leaves change colour, a deep richness can be seen in the barks of the trees; the landscape starts to look barren and empty, transforming the warm beauty of the summer into the cold, sharp, naked beauty of winter.

The calf was now a big lump of an animal and would fill twice over the small car in which it was brought home. All my father's animals were treated as pets, he would call each one by name, and they always responded. Hay was stored for the winter; bags of sawdust from the pit sawmill were fetched and stored, rushes that had been cut and dried in the summer were packed into the loft and around the cowshed, until needed, and covered with felt to protect against the rain. Everything was ready for winter. The garden waste was burned and spread, manure was distributed over the garden ready for the next planting, in the spring.

The next event to look forward to was bonfire night and fireworks. There would be fires everywhere. Weeks before, we were on the look out for anything that would burn: old logs, trees, old mattresses and furniture, all found its way to the bonfire heap, ready for the big night. We spent all our money on bangers, and sparklers, the ones you held in your hand as the twinkling sparks sprayed all over the place. My uncle Jack, in spite of objections from my parents, made sure I had enough money for dozens of bangers that year.

My uncle was now my good friend, and you do not squeal on friends. We had a code that only we knew: three half winks meant our secret was safe, two winks warned us to be careful, and one wink meant: run like hell, your mother is on the warpath. Make yourself scarce until the coast is clear. As the day got nearer, the excitement built. A box of rainbow fireworks was already in the house, and my father was the only one who would let them off. He never knew about all the bangers I had stashed over the last few weeks; these would be let off by me later, after my father and mother had gone into the house, to have a cup of tea and a bite to eat.

Jack was in his wheelchair, wrapped up to the neck in warm clothes, with a cap stuck firmly on his head. He could have passed for the Guy, with all the clothes wrapped around him, except that, every time we looked at each other, he gave three winks, or two, according to where my mother was, but never one, and so I knew I was safe.

Mog was there, interfering in everything and not worrying whether anyone cared. Even if they did, he paid no attention. He would light a cigarette, place it in Jack's mouth, light another one, and put it between his own lips, where it would stay until it was too small to hold. Every minute or so, he would take the cigarette out of Jack's mouth, shake the ash off it and place it back into his mouth, almost mechanically. As soon as one cigarette went out, another would be lit and the process would go on.

The bonfire would be roaring, the sound of wood cracking and hissing could be heard clearly, as the flames shot upward in the cold night sky. The warmth from the fire could be felt against the face as flames glowed in all colours against the dark background of the night and the coal tips. The smell of smoke was everywhere and got into the nostrils and down the throat, but we were happy, it was part of the fun. Potatoes were wrapped in tin foil and placed over a nearby bin filled with coal, lit for the occasion, away from the main bonfire.

The men had hip flasks full of whisky or brandy, and would pass the flask around surreptitiously, when the women were not looking. They knew exactly what was going on but turned a blind eye. The colours would be all around us as the different fireworks went off. Skyrockets would light up the night sky, loud bangs were heard overhead as the cascade of colours exploded and covered the sky. We would be shouting, laughing, eating, and sharing our feelings and the excitement of the moment, a community together, every person playing a part in the never-ending circle of life.

Over the coming weeks, Jack and I became ever closer, and we spent many hours talking and sharing our experiences. He was in increasing pain and it was sometimes so intense that extra painkillers were needed. These made him drowsy and he would be talking to me one minute and asleep the next. I would sit by his side and watch him sleep, hoping he would wake up and be able to resume our conversation. His arms were thin and he was losing weight daily. The doctor called a few times a week and tried his best the make Jack as comfortable as possible, but it was becoming obvious that he would have to go into hospital if things did not improve.

My father was worried. I could see in his eyes that, for all his effort, even he knew he was losing this great battle and there was nothing he could do about it. He spent time alone, often going for a walk, to collect his thoughts. He would tell me, as he ruffled my hair, "Life is a hard taskmaster and will always have its way. We are but its pawns, and life plays with us as sport."

These words were spoken with tremendous feeling and his face wore a sad expression. My father was now starting to come to terms with the inevitable. There was no hope for Jack, and this was hard for his brother to accept. I could feel the hurt in my father and so much wished to help him, but I, too, was helpless against the fates.

"I love my uncle, daddy. He is kind and my friend."

I meant every word. My father held me in his arms.

"He is a true friend to you, my son, but his pain and suffering are getting worse and there is not a thing anyone can do to help."

"I am sorry for the way I felt. When I saw my uncle first, he frightened me and seemed like a cabbage, always in one place and needing everything done for him, like a baby. Can you please forgive me for my thoughts, daddy?"

I looked away as I spoke these words.

"I told you a few months ago that there is nothing to forgive. You have a right to feel as you did." my father said, lovingly.

"I love him, daddy, and do not feel the same way now. I want my uncle to live, not die. He is my friend."

"My boy, I always knew you would feel a deep love for your uncle, in time."

This confused me. How could my father know that I would change my mind? I asked him. He told me to sit next to him; he placed his arm around my shoulder, as only a father can, and spoke the most valuable words I have ever heard from another person.

"When the heart is touched with love and friendship, the eyes become blind to all imperfections. The infirmity of the body is not important; it becomes an irrelevance, when two souls touch each other in kindness, tolerance and love."

He pulled his pipe from his pocket, placed in into his mouth, lit it and puffed for a few seconds, before he carried on with the conversation.

"The frail body we are born into, my son, is continually reconstructed by a replica of itself, many times throughout our life, and is no more than the shell we are born into. The only continuity we have is in our soul. A beautiful and pure soul is often hidden in a deformed body, and to stop there and see only the deformity in all its ugly nakedness and pain is to deprive yourself of the main jewel of life, the attractiveness of an uncontaminated and good soul. Look behind the pain and suffering to see the beauty below the surface; do not stay on the outside, but enter deep into the person and share the pureness of the depth below."

I could not say a word for a few seconds and then asked again, "How did you know I would feel love for my uncle?"

"How do we know grass will grow or the sun will shine? You just know. You both have good souls; there could only be one outcome. I knew you would love each other, over time. There was only ever one outcome."

I knew now why my father had not been perturbed by my initial reaction to my Uncle Jack.

Christmas was almost upon us. The house was decorated to the full that year. A Christmas tree took over the whole corner of the room, leaving very little space in which to move around. The tree was covered all over with twinkling lights, little toys, chocolate and sweets, and tinsel, and had a fairy stuck on the top. Every Christmas, I felt glad not to be a fairy, because I would never get used to a tree branch permanently wedged up my bottom, and I wondered why everyone needed a fairy on the top of the Christmas tree. Every year, there it would be, a silver wand in its hand, a permanent smile on its face, surveying the room.

The weather was bitterly cold, with a sharp wind that blew down the valley. Windows and doors were shut tight, rags were wedged into any gap in the doors and windows, to keep the cold air out. My mother did her bit by permanently bellowing at the top of her voice, her power lifting the temperature in the house with each word spoken. My father would call her an extra fire, always glowing, her warmth filling the whole house. Her lungs would be full open, when she was shouting to anyone in earshot, and that meant the whole street.

"Close all doors and wear a scarf around the neck at all times if you are going out."

Just to be on the safe side, everyone wore a scarf around their neck all the time, even Jack, and he was tucked up in bed like a Christmas Turkey, bedclothes up around his neck, the scarf clearly visible. The slightest sound in the house would start her off shouting, even when all the doors and windows were tightly closed and we had no intention of venturing out of doors. The inside of our windows would have permanent condensation dripping off them, and I was convinced that it was the hot air my mother generated hitting the inside of the glass and turning to water.

The first of the winter snow started to fall at the beginning of December, and everyone thought we should have a white Christmas. The rooftops of the long terraced houses looked like the tops of little peaks. The only places not covered by snow were the two monstrosities that were forever vying for most obnoxious object. The snow could not bring itself to land and stay on these monuments to exploitation for even a minute, but melted immediately upon impact. It was as if these blights on the landscape enjoyed spoiling the picturesque Christmas scene; one billowing smoke, the other coughing up grease and dirt; as the large, black wheel moved around in a never-ending circle, in homage to its God: Black Gold.

All around, the land was white and clean; the black coal tips were transformed, as if by magic, into White Mountains that took on a whole new beauty. Black covered in white, a surface altered first by man was transformed now by the forces of Nature. Even the river was cleaner, the coal dust and rubble temporarily frozen and unable to enter the once pure water.

The children came out in force, the snow acting as a magnet. Snowmen were built, with carrots for noses, stones for eyes, sticks for ears, combs for mouths. The snowmen were knocked down, rebuilt, knocked down again, in a cycle of fun. All the children, wrapped in caps, scarves, gloves and coats of all colours, went rushing here and there, coats covered in snow, their breath steaming.

As the big day approached, my father increased the feed for the cockerels and turkeys. He could earn a few pounds for Christmas by taking orders from the neighbours for turkeys and chickens for the traditional Christmas lunch. Eggs were produced all the year round, and the sale of them to the neighbours helped towards the cost of grain to feed the birds, and to cover the cost of holidays. Christmas was the main earning period, but the preparation would be intense.

For a week before they were due to be killed, the birds were confined to the chicken pens, and not allowed to roam about the garden. Kept well fed until a day before they were to be killed; on the last day of their lives, all food would be removed, leaving only water for them to drink. There would be upwards of forty chickens and an equal number of turkeys to be slaughtered and cleaned ready for the oven, before Christmas.

The Saturday before Christmas, my father and I were up early, to prepare for the work that would take the whole of the weekend. My mother had plenty of hot water available, and the old tin bath was placed at the bottom of our steps, ready to receive the birds. This was a job I disliked intensely, but it had to be completed in two days, so there was no time to reflect on the right or wrong of the situation. Christmas was upon us and we needed to eat. The birds were our food, and the act that we were about to perform had been repeated many times, from the time of early man until the present day, fathers helped by sons.

Jack said, when we spoke about the slaughter, "I remember as if it were yesterday, my father, your grandfather, preparing in the same way. We always killed a pig in addition to the poultry for Christmas."

He smiled as he recollected how things were, all those years ago, in number 12, Park Road, the place of his birth and where his character was shaped as a young lad.

"It was a part of our way of life, as it had been for generations long gone; it was our way of surviving." These were his last few words as he drifted off to sleep that night.

We were up at six o'clock that morning, and went straight to the pens. The chickens and cockerels were caught first. Their legs were tied together and the birds were placed into a sack. When the sack was full, my father sat on a stool and I handed one of the tied birds to him. Taking the bird in his hands, he placed its head between his knees, held the body under his arm and, with one clean movement, jerked the head downward until the neck broke. The break was always clean and quick, to minimize the bird's suffering. The body would flap and shake, and he would hang the bird upside down on a nail in the side of the garden shed. This process was repeated until the bag was empty.

All the dead birds were hanging from the shed in a line, some still moving and jerking as the bodies cooled, bleeding slightly from the beak, eyes glazed in death. Their wings hung open, flapping slightly as we placed them into sacks, to carry home, to be cleaned and prepared for the table.

The dead birds were placed into the tin bath; boiling water was poured over them and my father would start to pluck the feathers, leaving the remains in the water. Next, the birds were placed on a large, flat stone slab, waist high, in the back garden. The heads were removed, necks cleaned, and the giblets removed. The giblets were cooked and given to the dogs. The bird would be washed under running water and left on the table to dry. The unwanted feathers and the other waste would be dug into a hole in the garden, for fertilizer.

This work continued throughout the day. The turkeys would share same fate, after the chickens were finished. Distribution to the customers took all evening. Mog and Davy, a few other people that were having a bad time that year, and a small number of the older neighbours would all be given a bird, with a few potatoes, carrots, and a cabbage thrown in for good measure.

For a child, Christmas Eve is a time of extreme excitement and anticipation. Memories of Christmases spent when you are young stay with you forever. There is a magic in the air; Christmas is here, the presents are imminent, the waiting is almost over.

There would always be a lot going on, and last minute preparations continued the whole day. Our house was a hive of activity, everyone on the go, but not a lot being achieved. My mother would be busy baking cakes and cooking the meat and turkey. This task would always be completed the night before. My father cleaned the vegetables and put them in saucepans, for boiling the following day. Everything had to be concluded now, because no work would be done on the next day, which was a time of relaxation and enjoyment.

Presents and chocolates were just a day away. The sooner we went to bed that night, the sooner it would be Christmas. Carol singing was heard in the streets and it echoed along the valley floor. Strong Welsh voices could be heard, all singing together in harmony, the singers wrapped up in caps, scarves, coats and gloves, some with candle lights in jars, others held torches. Others, with carol sheets in hand, stamped their feet on the snow, to keep warm, everyone happy and merry, enjoying the festive season.

Our house was open to all. Mince pies were on the table, a bottle of whisky close by, plenty of tea in the pot. There was a steady flow of neighbours and friends coming in and out, more so this year because a lot of Jack's friends also called, to wish him a Happy Christmas. The fire in the grate was piled high with coal, the glow from the open flames projecting the warmth into the whole room. The whisky moved steadily down the bottle, to be replaced by another bottle, when it was empty. There were also a few bottles of beer. Christmas was a time of sharing, and if we had it, we shared it, as other people had shared with us, when we were having a hard time.

The local pub would be full on Christmas Eve, and the beer pumps in constant use, to pull pint after pint. The colliers knew how to party. Jack was taken down to the pub in his wheelchair and placed in a corner next to the coal burning stove, near to the bar, that was now recognized as his spot.

The toilet was at the far end of the room and was in continual demand. It would have been easier for most of the men in the bar to stay in the toilet and have the beer brought to them. No sooner had they left this little room, than they would be back, washing the walls again. It seemed to be a waste of precious time, to keep going from the bar to the toilet and back again.

Everyone in the room was talking at the same time, smoke thick in the air, everyone contributing its own bit of pollution into the room. The ashtrays were overflowing with cigarette stubs; the stone floor littered with ash and discarded cigarette ends. No one paid the slightest attention, and even if they did, they were indifferent to the polluted atmosphere. This was clean to them, when compared to the air underground. They were there to enjoy the evening and that is all that mattered on Christmas Eve.

Continual laughter was the air. One of the men would jump up on a chair and start to sing, followed by the rest of the drinkers. A few of the older folk, playing cards and dominoes in the far corner, would complain that they were unable to concentrate on the game. This just incited everyone to sing louder, until the card and domino players joined in, shaking their heads in disgust at the noise, but smiling to themselves. At closing time, a steady stream of men flowed out of the pub, in high spirits, singing to high heaven as they began the trek home. They were all unsteady on their feet, moving two steps forward, one step backwards, and another sideways.

Mog sang any words that came into his head. The rest of the merry congregation did likewise, all singing to their own tune, each one thinking he was the one in tune. To prove it, they raised their voices higher, unsuccessfully trying to drown out the rest. Jack sang with the rest. They could have been taken for citizens of Babel; they were unintelligible to everyone but themselves, and not one of the men was able to walk a straight line or speak without a slur.

The streetlight at the corner of number 13 Park Road was the gathering place for the singing somnambulists. Some stood against the light pole; others sat on the front wall, near to the lamppost, or were lying in the snow, oblivious to the cold. The men were happy, without a care in the world, and King Coal was forgotten for tonight.

As further neighbours joined the happy cluster, Mog popped indoors for a bottle of whisky, which would be handed around the group. The streetlight reflecting against the snow made the people look like silhouettes against the whiteness. The wives were at home, trying to get the children off to sleep, and prepare for the following day, but the noise outdoors was enough to wake the dead, and so the children had no chance of falling asleep. My father was one of those in the group, singing for all his worth. Mog, by this time, could barely speak and had difficulty remaining on his feet, let alone standing up straight. There were Dai Buck, Mog, Ron, Trevor, Glyn and my father, all holding each other up, swaying constantly, occasionally falling over as if playing ring a ring a roses, and laughing all the more when this happened. The only one that did not fall over that night was Jack, because he was already sitting down.

When my mother had had enough of all the commotion, she marched over to the assembled crowd, a full bucket of cold water in hand. She threw the icy water over the chorus, which was enough to elicit a sudden response. A loud shout was heard as one of the party fell over and took the rest down with him into the snow.

My mother stood over them, hands on hips, face red with anger, finger pointing menacingly, and shouting at them at the top of her voice, to keep the noise down, but making more noise in the process.

"Get in this house now, Dai. The rest of you, get home and get to sleep. Have you no beds to go to?" she raged. "You are all like a lot of wailing cats, and if you behave in this manner, it will not be water I will be throwing over you next time, but the piss pot."

This undoubtedly had the required response and it was not long before the party dispersed and went indoors. The thought of a full piss pot over their heads did not in the least appeal to them, drunk as they were.

The next morning, as usual, my father was the first to rise. He would see to Jack's toiletries and exercises, and make a cup of tea and take it upstairs for my mother. Today, the tea would be special, as my father would term it; there would be a shot of brandy in the cup. This was a tradition in our house, from as far back as I am able to remember, but it only happened on Christmas morning. The fire was raked and made up with coal, and he prepared a fried breakfast of bacon, eggs, black pudding and fried bread for us all.

We sat down together and wished each other a merry Christmas. Soon, the neighbours started to call and wish us a happy Christmas. Mog was one of the first and he would have his tea with an extra helping of brandy.

"Here you are, Mog, have this," my mother said lovingly, as she poured a good helping of brandy into his cup. "Drink it up; there is more where that came from."

Christmas dinner that year was extra special because it was shared with Jack. We all knew that this would be Jack's last Christmas, and we went out of our way to make it extra special. My father stood up, a glass in hand.

"Happy Christmas to you all," he said, looking at Jack. They both knew, but would not dare say aloud, that this would be the last Christmas they would spend together on this earth. "May God protect us all for another Christmas, and to those that are less fortunate than we are, may good luck fall upon them all; to my brother Jack." He raised his glass to my uncle. "Our life has been enriched these last few months by your company, and no one knows what is in store for us, but the memories of the last few months, and especially today, will be locked in my heart forever. To you, Jack, my brother."

Jack did not say a word for a few moments, just stared straight at my father and then said, in an affectionate voice full of deep emotion, "Your place in heaven is already secured. May God protect you, Dai."

The presents were opened, everyone was happy with their surprises; socks, aftershave, soap, and underpants were the most frequent gifts. Everybody claimed to have received just what they wanted. My main present that year was a bike with drop handlebars, three gears, a pouch on the bars for a water bottle, and a bag on the end of the seat, for spanners and small parcels. By the night-time, after the excitement of the day, we were all tired. After a turkey sandwich with lashings of Branston pickle, we were all in bed before eleven o'clock.

Boxing Day saw empty boxes over the whole house, presents left under chairs or on the floor. Everything had to be put away in the cupboards until required. After breakfast, Glyn came over to stay with Jack, and we all went down Chepstow Road to see my grandmother, Dave, Peg and their young daughter, baby Karen, who was similar in age to my younger brother and just as much trouble.

We arrived in Chepstow just after midday and settled down to have a cup of tea at the back of the house, where mam mam, my grandmother, lived. Dave and Peg occupied the middle room with the baby; the front room was the best room and only used on very rare occasions. There was an open fire in the middle of the room where mam mam lived, and by the side of the fire was a black kettle next to a teapot, that could be put to use at a moment's notice. The teapot was forever being topped up with hot water from the continually boiling kettle, with the occasional spoonful of fresh tea from the caddy on the mantelpiece above the fire added for good measure.

Presently, Mog arrived, together with Nan and Doug and their son Barry, and a few other relatives, and we would all be squashed in together, drinking tea and eating cake and biscuits. Dave popped in with bottles of beer and handed them round the room.

"There are plenty more where these came from. Do not be shy and stand on ceremony. They must all be drunk," he said.

Mam-mam was forever bending over the fireplace, topping up the teapot. The room would be full to bursting with her children and relatives, all talking together about everything and nothing. No sooner was a cup empty than it was filled again. To leave a cup empty, for even a few seconds, was to be avoided at all costs.

The smoke in the room was thick enough to cut with a knife.

If you stopped drinking tea, you were expected to eat: welsh cakes, Christmas cake, biscuits and sandwiches of all descriptions were laid out on the table, with a constant reminder from mam mam that they must be eaten, or they would go waste. To refuse would be futile; another piece of food would be handed to you, and often placed into your mouth, if your hands did not respond at the required speed. Resistance was not an alternative.

As time passed, the laughter grew louder, and time seemed to move faster as the evening approached. Most of the men were 'well oiled', as my grandmother would say, pleased that everyone was having a good time. When it was time to return home, all left together, the men calling into the Legion on the way, to wish the occupants a Happy Boxing Day, or so they would have us believe.

Chapter 16

THAT NIGHT, JACK was in constant pain, and the doctor was called and arrived within the hour. Jack's whole body was in continuous movement, and he could not stop shaking. An injection was administered and, after a few minutes, his muscles relaxed and he went into a deep sleep. The doctor called again the following day, and had a word with both my parents. After he left, there was a look of despair on both their faces. My father went in to look at Jack and sat beside him, not saying a word. My mother asked me to leave my father alone with Jack, wrap up warm and go out to play.

On New Year's Eve, every year, there was a party in our house. There was plenty of drink left after Christmas, and a barrel of beer and extra bottles would be purchased from the Tremains Hotel and placed in the lean-to at the rear of the house. On the day of the party, the carpets were taken up and removed upstairs. My mother would never risk beer being spilt over the carpets. The oilcloth could be cleaned easily with soap and water in the morning. There was open house and everyone was invited to the celebrations, which lasted most of the night. The only concern was for Jack, but he was looking forward to the event and assured us that the noise and partying would be just what he needed to keep him in high spirits.

All the men spent the early evening in the pub; some would venture down to the Legion or the Park Hotel, but would all end up in the Tremains by about ten thirty. My father went no further than the Tremains as he still had Jack, resting at home, much in his mind. Mog turned up at about ten o'clock, swaying unsteadily, after calling in at the Legion and the Park Hotel on the way up to the Tremains. The party would start to get under way at about ten o clock, and there was an unwritten rule in our house, that the whole family must be together to see in the New Year; my father insisted upon this and it remained a custom in our house, even when we were all a lot older.

The first to arrive, at about eleven, was my father, happy and smiling. His first task was to see to Jack and settle him in the wheelchair. Afterwards, we waited for the Television to announce that the New Year had arrived. Glasses would be filled with beer or wine, and at the first stroke of twelve, we would all see the New Year in and the old year out, hold hands, and sing *Old Lang Syne,* kissing, hugging and holding each other after the song was finished. My father would then make another speech, with which we were all familiar, and say, "May God keep us all safe for another year," lift the glass to his mouth and toast, 'the family', and we would all drink, 'to us'.

Now the neighbours would appear, and the men from the pub in ones and twos, singing and wishing everyone a Happy New Year. The children also wished everyone the same and held out their hands for a few coppers. My mother had a large jar of sweets by the door, and gave them out to anyone that wished her a Happy New Year.

I was under strict instructions not to drink any alcohol, the only taste allowed was during the toast, and this increased my curiosity to try beer and wine. The large barrel in the lean-to was propped up against the wall, on a bench placed there for the purpose. A curtain was placed around the bottom, to hide the wood, and on the floor was a tray to collect the spillage when the glasses were filled. The men went back and forth all the time, to replenish their glasses. There was just enough room for the barrel and for one person to stand beside it. This gave me the opportunity I was looking for, and I worked out my strategy, to taste the contents of the cask and not get caught. Directly under the barrel was a space, into which I crept, covered from view by the curtain. I placed a cushion on the floor directly under the barrel. I fetched a plate full of food and a glass, waited until the coast was clear, and went out of sight, under the barrel. I could see through a gap in the curtain whether the coast was clear. I filled the glass from the tray on the floor, and drank. The first taste seemed agreeable, and it was not long before my hand crept out from under the curtain for a refill. This went on for a while, as I was slowly diminishing the plate of food, until I could not eat or drink any more.

My head started to spin, slowly at first, but increasing as the minutes ticked away. I did not feel merry, nor in singing mood, but giddy and nauseous. This was not supposed to happen. The rest of the party people were in high spirits, very much alive, and singing on the top of their voices, and they had been drinking all night.

Our cat came looking for a quiet place, away from the crowd and out of the cold. It moved behind the curtain with me and sat on my lap, purring and meowing, happy to see me, glad that it, too, had found this secluded corner. I could see two pairs of cat's eyes, and they could not keep still, but seemed to move in a circle, round and round, never stopping, but moving ever faster.

This became too much for the sandwiches, crisps, sweets and the drink that I just consumed. They could not stay in my stomach. The eyes had startled them into action, and the food insisted on meeting the two pairs of moving eyes as quickly as possible, totally against my better judgment. The contents of my stomach speedily came up to meet them in one sharp movement, and I deposited the whole mixture over the moving cat's eyes.

The cat's eyes moved no more. They could not be seen. The animal was covered from the tip of the nose to the end of the tail. The purring and meowing turned to a howl of shock and disgust. There was no sense of forgiveness here. The cat froze rigid for a moment, then, jumped up, knocking his head in the process on the top of the platform we were hiding under, and gave one almighty roar, before running out from under the barrel and into the other room.

This could not be explained away with any conviction; my cover had been blown, and I needed to think fast if I was to get out of this situation. The trail the cat left could clearly be seen, and the smell was now starting to become apparent. I needed divine intervention to turn this to my advantage, and I found it in my good old Uncle Jack.

Crawling out from under the curtain, with the assembled crowd looking on and waiting for an explanation I did not have, my only defence was to throw myself at the mercy of the crowd and accept the punishment. Jack was the first to speak.

"I told you that if you were feeling ill you had to tell your parents; they would understand, not hide under the curtain until you were feeling better in case you spoilt the party. You are such a considerate lad."

My reply was quick.

"I did not wish to spoil the party, and crawled into the corner so as not to disturb any one. I'm sorry I felt ill, and made all this mess, but it really was not my fault, I think I ate too much turkey. I crawled under the curtain so as not to be any trouble, but was disturbed by the cat; he jumped on my stomach. Can you forgive me, please, for making all this mess?"

"What a considerate boy he is, to think this way," one of the guests commented, with concern in her voice.

Another chipped in, "He is far too considerate for his age, to show such concern for other people. He really is a good boy."

I was looking like a little cherub, eyes sparkling, hands down behind my back, displaying a curl across my forehead, looking as if butter would not melt in my mouth. My mother was not totally convinced, and looked at me in a strange way at first but, eventually, gave me the benefit of the doubt, and after a while, she hugged me for being so considerate, cleaned up the mess, and gave me a change of clothes.

I turned my eyes to my uncle when the coast was clear, and he gave me three winks, to signify that the explanation had been accepted and there was no one on my case. My luck had held out against the odds. I acknowledged the help with a nod of the head, went over to him and gave him a hug. I whispered a thank you, and touched his head with both hands.

The cat was shuffled out of the door to shouts of disapproval for jumping on my stomach when I was not feeling well. The general consensus was that he deserved what he got, for being so uncaring and thoughtless and jumping on my stomach. Every time the cat saw me after that, I was convinced he had one eye on my mouth, even when he was asleep by the fireplace. The new relationship was always one of caution. He would not be the 'fall cat' again if he could help it, and he kept firmly off my lap.

The party went on until the dawn came and the guests slowly drifted away. The last few remaining were treated to a fried breakfast, and then everyone went home to bed, to sleep off the over-indulgence of the night. The party had been a great success and would be talked about for the next few months. The cat became a story in itself.

Chapter 17

A T TWELVE-O-CLOCK on New Year's Day, after only a few hours sleep, Mog called me up from bed, to walk down to Chepstow Road, to wish mam mam a Happy New Year. This was the only time of the year when we walked the main road, and not the back lane. There were many stops on the way. Mog knew the whole population of Cwmparc and collected all the gossip on the way down.

By the time we arrived at our destination I had accumulated a pocket full of coins. Every person we met wished us a Happy New Year, and Mog always pointed to me and said, "Give the boy a few coins; it will bring you luck."

The next few days saw a further decline in Jack's health. When he was awake, we discussed many different topics. His main emphasis was on education and how this could be my pathway to success.

"Do not go the way of the miner and end up with a lung full of black dust. Take on the world and make your mark; guard against false counsel, and always follow your own instincts," he said.

"I want to follow the valley way and become a miner like all the rest of my family. I do not like school and wish I did not have to go to that horrible place. We are workers; why do we need to fill our minds with words and figures?" I protested, showing him my hands as if to reinforce the point that I am a worker.

"We are workers because we were forced to be; there was no choice. You have a choice. Do not waste the opportunity. Take on the world and win, but on your terms. Do not be an ant, always working to make someone else rich. Look on life as an apple tree and, providing you do not hurt anyone or exploit your fellow human beings, take the apples. The world will be yours to command and conquer. Please, promise me you will try. Well, what is your answer?"

"I will try." I responded, recognizing that my uncle's words could just as easily have come from my father.

The following day, the doctor was called again to Jack, and spent over an hour examining him. He concluded that the only hope, and it would be a slim one, was for him to go back into Stoke Mandeville Hospital, in Aylesbury, as soon as possible. He would not survive a car journey, and an ambulance was booked to transport him to Buckinghamshire.

The doctor's decision caused the whole household to go into shock. Jack had to go back into hospital; he could no longer survive at home. He needed all the facilities of a specialist hospital, and the one that specialized in this type of illness was Stoke Mandeville. The doctor returned that evening and told us that the ambulance would be at the door, the day after next, at nine in the morning, and to make sure that Jack was prepared for the journey.

"I will be here at seven o clock, before the ambulance arrives, to administer medication," the doctor said.

My father and Jack spent that evening together. If any visitors turned up, they were politely turned away and told that there would be plenty of time to see Jack on the following day. The brothers were in discussion for most of the evening, only interrupted when my mother brought cups of tea and sandwiches for my father.

The follow day, Jack seemed cheerful, and my father went out early in the morning, returning with Ron, his friend, and an old Transit van, big enough for a wheelchair. I thought for a moment that he would be taking Jack to hospital himself, but later realized he was taking Jack around the Valley, to see the sights.

They had obviously been discussing this the night before, and planned the journey at this time. Jack was not in a fit state to take this trip, and I said to my mother, "He should stay in bed, not tramp the valley. The doctor will be furious if he finds out."

"He obviously does not know. It is something that they both need to do. Jack is saying goodbye to the Valley. Leave them both alone, and wish them luck. The ground is covered and scarred, but it is their home, the only place they know. This journey is important to the two of them; it will be their last journey together in this Valley."

Jack was placed in the wheelchair, wrapped up well, and wheeled out to the van, where a few of the neighbours lifted him into the back. The snow was still around, but all the roads were clear. The weather was cold, grey low clouds covered the morning sky, periodically punctured by rays of sunshine as the winter sun broke through the cloud. They first travelled to the top of the Bwlch Mountain, stopping for Jack to look over his Valley below. From this point, you can see the terrace houses in their neat rows, and line upon line of slate roofs extending as far as the eye can see.

Tremains, the Park, and the Dare Collieries could be clearly seen, as well as the Fishing River and the Ragged Mountain in the forefront, majestically towering over the floor of the valley, and above them was the source of the river they both knew and had walked as children. This mountain would outlive the slag heaps that formed carbuncles on the mountainside. They stayed at this point for a while. None will ever know what was spoken between them as they looked over and down on the pits, river, houses and gardens. They may have spoken about their parents, or how the valley had changed from when they were young children, but this is speculation. What we do know is, they shared memories in each other's company, and that is all we need to know.

The next stop was the Rhigos. This mountain road runs via Treorchy and Treherbert, and winds around and up the mountain on one side, and descends the other, until it reaches the next valley, over the mountain in Hirwaun. They did not travel the whole mountain road, but just went high enough to look over the valley below. This is a spectacular sight. Larger than the valley they had just left, but equally spectacular and wonderful, it was all part of the Rhondda Valley they loved.

Jack was now tired but not yet ready to quit. There was one more place he needed to see before he was ready to be taken back to Cwmparc: his parents' grave in the cemetery at Treorchy. The emotions were running high as the van moved down off the mountain road and through Treherbert, until it turned left at the pub on the corner, to start the climb up the hill to the cemetery. The gates at the top were open and the van drove straight through, following the narrow road around the graves until it reached the one where their mother and father were buried.

The van stopped as close to the grave as possible and they both sat together, Jack in the back of the van, in the wheelchair, and his brother next to him. Ron left them there and walked away; he recognized that they needed to be alone with each other and their thoughts.

They stayed there for over half an hour, talking together and to the grave, as if the headstone would answer back. They felt that they were talking to their parents, and they did not see the cold stone staring back, but the warm loving faces of their parents, smiling at them, as they would have done many times in the past. Death has no power over love. Their parents' values and beliefs were firmly locked into the memory of these two individuals, burnt into their souls, and branded with love, from the time they were born, and would remain there for the rest of their lives. Both now felt lost, frightened, bewildered and needing reassurance that the future will be all right, even as the life of one was coming to a close.

"Dai, promise me that I will be buried with mam and dad. The grave will hold one more person." Jack spoke quietly, staring at the ground around the grave, knowing it would not be long before this earth would be over him, and his name on the cold headstone alongside those of his parents. "This will be my final resting place."

My father held Jack's hand, and they laughed, easing the tension of this solemn moment, when they both realized that there was no feeling in Jack's hands.

"Place your hands on my head, Dai, or hold my ear."

This resulted in further laughter.

"Come, it is time to go."

Ron was called and the three of them left the cemetery and headed home.

Jack was exhausted; the strain of the journey could be clearly seen. His eyes looked sunken, and swollen around the rims; his mouth quivered with nervous energy, his body twitched, but there was an inner glow visible on his face, as if he was congratulating himself on a job well done. He slept for most of the afternoon and, around five in the evening, visitors started to arrive. All the brothers turned up as well as a few of the neighbours and old friends, to wish him a safe journey and to ask when he would be coming back. The only answer he made to this question was, "Soon."

He knew that the span of his life was nearing its completion. This is what he meant when he told them he would be back soon. He meant he would be back for the funeral. That was to signal his release from his daily suffering. It was his way of saying goodbye forever to *his Valley* and its occupants. The significance of this remark was not lost on my father, and I could see the tears swell in his eyes as he excused himself to go to the garden to feed the animals. He needed to be alone for a while with his thoughts.

That night, after the visitors were gone, I sat by the side of my uncle until my mother shuffled me along to bed. Looking back as I went up the stairs, I saw that he was sound asleep, breathing heavily, every breath a little more difficult than the one before.

The next morning, I was up at six o'clock. The noise from the pit was always in the background. As I was coming down the stairs, I heard the siren go off, signalling the start of the day shift. It was still dark and the wind was whistling down the street, competing with the man-made sounds from the pit.

My father, who slept on a portable bed, was already up and sitting in a chair, in quiet and reflective mood. He looked at me, stood up, walked into the next room, went to the cupboard, made me a jam sandwich and handed it to me with a glass of milk. He smiled at me, went back into the other room, folded up the bed and carried it upstairs, returned and tended to Jack's toiletry needs and medications, all without speaking a single word.

A few minutes later, there was a knock on the front door. The doctor had arrived. He was shown into the room and given a cup of tea, as he went about preparing Jack for the long journey back to Aylesbury. Glyn, Mog and the two Jims, brother and cousin, turned up. The time was approaching for the ambulance to arrive, and Jack was all prepared and ready for the journey.

They say that the only constant in life is change, and things were about to change. I was to lose a friend and an ally, and I felt like shit on a warm day as the ambulance arrived and they carried Jack out on a stretcher. The last time I saw him, he was in obvious pain but trying to smile and face his destiny with dignity. He gave me three winks. I looked him in the face, smiled, and he was gone.

My father accompanied him to the hospital and returned the

following day, because he was working the night shift and needed to be back for work that evening. The ambulance turned at the corner of number twelve, and with a wave from the driver, it was on its way down Cwmparc. It went out of sight in a few minutes, taking my uncle out of my life forever, but never out of my mind.

I ran back into the house, trying to hide the tears flowing down my cheeks. Big boys do not cry. I ran upstairs and fell on my bed, sobbing and crying. I knew we would not see each other again, and this loss of a true friend and uncle was hurting me deep in the pit of my stomach. I no longer saw a paralysed man, unable to move, only a friend that I loved and had laughed with over the last few months.

My mother came into the room, and I ran into her arms and cried. She drew me to her side, put her arms around me and held me, as only a mother can when one of her brood is hurting.

"Why did Uncle Jack need to go away, mammy? I want him to stay."

"I know, my love. We all do, but he is very ill and in continuous pain. We cannot look after him any more, he is too ill. He needs constant attention if the pain is to be eased, and the only hospital specializing in this type of illness is in Aylesbury."

She brushed my tears away, picked up my hand and said, "Let us both go downstairs and clear up the room that Jack was in, and make it tidy before your father comes home tomorrow."

The following day, when my father returned, the room was already clear. Our household quickly returned to the way it had been before Jack's arrival. My parents were in regular contact with the hospital over the coming days, and there had been a slight improvement in Jack's condition. The spasms were a lot less frequent and there was an improvement in his skin condition. This news made us all feel a lot better and went some way to relieving the guilt about the surge of relief we all felt when he went back into hospital.

Chapter 18

I HAD BEEN NAGGING my father for a while about letting me keep a ferret and, each time the subject was broached, the answer was always, "No, wait until you are older."

A friend of mine, Deadeye Thomas, only a few months older than I, had already had a ferret for a while. I approached the subject again and, to my surprise, after a lecture on how to keep and look after the animal, my father agreed.

I built a hutch, lined on the outside with small chicken wire, as a precaution against the animal biting his way through the wooden planks and escaping. The hutch was placed inside a larger shed that once housed chickens, and I was ready to take delivery of my ferret.

This was the first live animal I was allowed to own. I kept mice in the back yard for a while, but they did not count because my mother had overall charge of them, and fed and cleaned them with me. This was to be a genuine pet, kept away from the house, and the responsibility for it was totally mine.

My father knew of a full-grown, white ferret for sale, and we went up to Vicarage Terrace, to look at the creature. After examining the animal and looking closely into its mouth and checking its feet, the purchase was concluded. My father had had a lot of experience with ferrets and knew exactly what to look for in a good one. As a young lad, he kept many ferrets, and often went rabbiting and ratting with his Uncle Harry, his father's brother, who lived with them at number twelve until he died.

The animal was soon safely in its new home, with sawdust on the floor and dried grass mixed with paper in its bedding area.

The hutch was just over two metres in length and about half a metre wide; with double thick wire mesh on the front and a door each end. Looking at this animal that now belonged to me made me really feel grown up, and proud that my father had the confidence in me to let me own it.

"Don't forget to feed it every day and make sure there is always fresh drinking water in the cage," my father instructed.

"Of course I will. The cage will be cleaned every day," I was swift to reply.

Having this animal was the best thing that ever happened, I felt at the time.

"You need to feed the animal on meat from the butcher. Go down to Mervyn and ask him if there is any dog meat for sale. Buy a pound or so. Here, take these few coppers to buy some." He had opened the cage and was stroking the animal. "Remember, these are fighting animals and they bite, so be careful, or you might lose the top of your finger. Get to know the creature and let him know your smell; he will not bite you if you handle him with care and kindness."

The ferret was placed back in the cage, the door locked, and we left, my father to go home, while I went down to the butcher's shop, to purchase the meat. On the way down, I called to see my friend Deadeye, to tell him the good news. I knew he would be down in his garden, near the front of his house. He was there, honing his shooting skills, looking for blackbirds or starlings, even the occasional cat, if it was dopey enough to walk over his garden. He was firmly of the opinion that they were trespassing and he was protecting his land against all comers. Even I had to shout and ask for permission to enter, when he was in hunting mood. Anything that moved was fair game to Deadeye, and the cockerel incident was still fresh in my mind.

I shouted, "Coming in. Do not shoot," and rushed to get behind him as soon as I could. He was very particular about his property and garden, and took it personally if any one uninvited strayed into his space. He was also of the opinion that, to be a real ferret keeper, you should not buy meat for the animal, but hunt your own in the form of blackbirds or starlings. Brian would spend hours in his garden, holed up behind some old corrugated tin sheet, a black bobble cap on head for camouflage, pellet gun in hand, and looking every inch the intrepid hunter waiting for his prey. To speak a word at these times was paramount to betrayal, and I would wait until his sentry duty was over before it was safe to speak.

"I have my own real live ferret," was my opening remark.

Always quick on the uptake, he asked, "Why, were you after a dead one?"

He put his gun down.

"A white one, full grown, and trained already to catch rats and rabbits." I excitedly boasted. This was not lost on him. He already had a polecat ferret, and a large one at that.

"You should have had one months ago and we could have trained them together," he replied quickly, looking to see if I had the animal with me. "Where is the ferret?"

"In the shed, settling down. I am going down to the butcher's, to get some food for it."

He looked at me in disgust, and said that he would come up my garden and shoot some food for the ferret. This I did definitely not want, I had visions of the cockerel, thanked him for his help, and refused. This made no difference. When he had something in his head, it seemed to connect with his whole body, rendering him deaf.

He picked up the gun, placed it under his arm, went to his hutch, collected his ferret, and placed it in a sack and into his inside pocket, which had been specially adapted for the purpose, and marched forward. In this mood, reasoning was out of the question. My only course of action was to hope we would not get into any trouble. This would not be easy. We walked up the hill from his garden, past the corner by his house, up the gully running by the side of the pit, past the Tremains Hotel, over the bombed houses near Treharn Street, and onto the side of the mountain to where the garden was, and where the ferret was housed.

He looked at my ferret with the trained eye of the hunter, picked up the animal with both hands, and examined its body closely, looking every bit the expert and connoisseur, and the ferret promptly bit him on his trigger finger. He shouted, screamed, shouted again, but the animal held firmly, until I grabbed its neck and held it until it opened is mouth.

His finger was bleeding profusely and the teeth marks could clearly be seen as the blood dripped over the intrepid hunter's clothes. He looked at all this blood and fainted, only to wake a few moments later and rush home to his mother in deep shock. I ran behind, a few minutes later, carrying his gun and shouting for him to stop. As I arrived at Barrett Street, his mother was already washing the finger and applying ointment to the affected spot, ready to cover it with a finger bandage. I left the gun in the passageway of the house and scampered off, before his mother could question me, and went on to the butcher's, which was my original plan at the start, feeling happy that the ferret was to eat meat from the butchers that afternoon, and I had managed to stay out of trouble.

The weather was still cold. Jack had been in hospital for just over two weeks, and there was no deterioration in his overall condition. This made us feel happy and my father suggested we all take a trip to see him, in a few weeks time, and stay near the hospital. Deep down, my father did not think he would see Jack alive again, and this made him very happy and excited about the prospect of going to Aylesbury. I had never been there before, indeed, I had never been outside Wales, and to see my uncle and friend again made me excited and happy.

"When are we going, daddy? Can I take my ferret to show Uncle Jack," I asked expecting my father to say yes.

"The hospital will not let it in, and the animal will became stressed by the journey, so the answer is no."

I was going to plead but the look on his face said it all, and there was no point, so I let the subject drop and did not mention it again.

The next Saturday morning, I got up early and went over my uncle Mog's house. He had a wire run and was going to adapt it from holding chickens to a run for the ferret. We would connect a hole from the cage into the run, to allow the ferret more space and give it an area in which to feed, allowing the cage to remain clean. The structure was in pieces, and we intended to modify it in his back garden and then move the whole structure up to our garden and connect it to the ferret cage.

He was waiting for me, and made me a fried breakfast, before starting work.

"There is no rush; we have all day," he said.

He could see my impatience, but you would not rush Mog; he had one speed, Mog's speed, and this would change according to the mood he was in and how he perceived the job.

After breakfast he would go to the toilet at the end of the garden, to contemplate the day to come and to have a quiet fag, as he would term the situation. I knew he would be at least another half hour before we would start. When he went up to the little house, he would be there for the duration.

"I am going to the small room, my haven at the end of the garden, my little throne room of total satisfaction and deep contemplation, where I can consider the job and reflect on the day to come," he would say, fag in mouth, newspaper in hand, as he went up the garden to the toilet.

He first read the newspaper, then ripped it into squares and placed these on a nail in the toilet door, for use as toilet paper.

"This new fangled paper in rolls is for babies' bottoms and women, not men." He would go to the toilet, read the paper, realize a page was missing, and shout at the top of his voice,

"Anne, page six is missing. Where the hell is this page?" Matters would immediately be put right and the disturbance to his tranquillity instantaneously rectified.

I would be given the missing sheet, rush it to my uncle, who was now shouting continually for the offending missing page. The sheet would be handed under the toilet door, and the contemplation would go on for another ten minutes, or three cigarettes, which ever came first. The toiletries over, the work would start.

The first and practically the only tool he had confidence in was the hammer. For the next few hours, he banged and knocked nails into the construction, pulling bits of wood across other bits of wood and nailing them together, until the whole lot held firmly, and the transformation from chicken coop to ferret run was complete.

It was now lunchtime, and a shout came from inside the house, telling us to wash our hands because dinner was on the table. My aunty could make a splendid bowl of stew, which we devoured like two hungry wolves. Second helpings were compulsory, as soon as the first was finished. Two platefuls later, we would be bursting and unable to manage another mouthful, and my aunty would be pleased. We were fed to excess. Mog sat in his chair by the fireplace, closed his eyes for a while, to let the food digest, and smoked a cigarette, before he was ready to resume the work.

The only thing left to do now was to carry the ferret run to where my hutch was; and we enlisted the help of a few of the neighbours for this task. No one could say no to Mog. It is always easier to comply with the request than to refuse, so there was no trouble in getting help.

A while later, the task completed, Mog handed cigarettes all round, as a thank you, and the neighbours returned to what they were doing earlier. The run was attached to the hutch and the job was complete. We were now well into Saturday afternoon, and the distant call of the Legion was beckoning Mog to its altar. This pull had the force of a strong magnet, and it was not long before he went to pay homage. I stayed with my ferret for a while, and went home at teatime.

Chapter 19

PREPARATIONS WERE getting under way for the visit to Aylesbury, and we needed an inexpensive place to stay, near the hospital. My father had been working double shifts since he decided to go, in order to have the money for the trip. He was working the morning shift and the afternoon shift, which meant he was not home until late evening, and back at work by six o clock the following morning. It was from work to bed and back to work, with no time in between. He made not the slightest complaint and there was always a smile on his face.

It was my job to feed all the animals, and I was up early in the morning, to see to them, before I went to school. In the evening, after tea, I did everything again, made sure the chickens were safely secure in the pens, and the cattle all fed and watered.

A few days before we were due to travel, a telegram was delivered to our house at five in the afternoon.

"Jack, ill, not responding to treatment."

My father was at work until ten that evening. My mother was sitting down when he entered the room, and he knew there was something wrong. My mother pointed to the table where the telegram was lying open from the time it was first read. He looked at it, placed in into his pocket, sat down, lit his pipe and stared at the wall for a few minutes, not speaking a word.

"We will go tomorrow, after I work the day shift. We will catch the next train or bus after three in the afternoon. Could you sort out the time of the journey tomorrow, Lol, before I come home from work?"

He spoke without emotion, in a quiet, reserved tone, as if he were talking to himself.

"It will be done, Dai," replied my mother.

The next morning, my mother rose early, to discuss the arrangements and the journey with my father, before he went to work. She arranged everything so that, immediately he arrived home, everything would be ready. My younger brother was to be left with Mair for a few days, and the rest of us would travel to Aylesbury. If we caught the four o'clock train from Treorchy, we would be in Cardiff before five, in time to catch the connecting train.

Cases were packed and left by the front door in readiness. She intended to catch the nine o'clock bus from Cwmparc, to buy the train tickets at Treorchy Station. The accommodation was to be arranged afterwards, by means of the station's telephone.

At eight thirty in the morning, my mother was sitting down to have a cup of tea before catching the bus to Treorchy, when there was a knock at the door. Standing in the cold, holding a telegram, was the postman. My mother signed for the letter and closed the door. She knew what the contents would say, and just placed it on the table, lit a cigarette and sat down.

"Hurry up, mummy; it is nearly nine o'clock and the bus is coming up the street."

"There will be no travel for us, today, or any other day," she said, and stubbed out the freshly lit cigarette in the ashtray.

"Daddy will not be happy if we cannot go because you have not collected the tickets," I warned.

My mother picked up the letter, opened it, read the contents and showed it to me.

"See. This is the reason: your uncle is no more."

I read the letter and placed it back on the table, slowly unfolding all the creases as I continued to look at the words.

I often heard the saying that the pen is mightier than the sword. I felt the power of them both at that moment. Each word drilled into my eyes, penetrating all the way into the brain. My Uncle Jack was dead. The telegram contained only seven words:

"Jack died at six this morning, sorry."

Tears started to fill my eyes, and the only word I could hold in my mind was 'sorry'. It shocked me, that single word of apology for the fact that he was no longer in this world. My mind jumped again. I could see him smiling through all his pain. I shall see his three winks no more; they were gone forever, we were left only with *sorry*.

My father walked through the door, looked at my mother, and without a word passing between them, all the words he would ever need to know were in my mother's eyes.

"You have been crying, Reen. The trip to London is off?"

"There is a telegram on the table. Jack died early this morning."

He shook his head, sat down next to my mother, placed his hand on her arm and said, "It is for the best. We said our goodbyes a few weeks ago. He was ready to go, and had had enough of all the pain and suffering. If the truth be known, he was looking forward to moving on."

"But, Dai, we were all going to see Jack, and now he is dead." Tears flowed down her face.

"We both knew he would not have long to live, and if we could see him again, as we planned, I would have been happy, but it was not to be."

He stood up, walked calmly out the door and up the garden, to spend the afternoon alone with his thoughts. This was a moment for which my father had prepared, and seemed to accept the situation with supreme calmness. When he returned, he started to prepare for his brother's body to be brought home, for the funeral that was to be from number twelve, the place of his birth.

The funeral took place a few days later, and the whole street turned out to say goodbye. The weather was dry but cold as he was buried with his parents, reunited in death with the two people he loved and who gave him life but expected nothing in return. After the funeral, there was a party at the Tremains Hotel. Jack had given money to my father to pay for everyone to have a few drinks at his funeral, and this is precisely what did happen. The beer flowed all afternoon and late into the night, as they wished Jack a quick and speedy journey into his next life. If the quantity of beer consumed were to be the measurement of his journey, he would already have arrived before the day was out, skiing on a tidal wave of best bitter.

The funeral over, life returned to normal. Winter was now well advanced and we were looking forward to the spring and the warmer weather. Jack was confined to my memory, and whenever I recalled his three winks, they always brought a smile to my face.

Chapter 20

I WAS GROWING OLDER and starting to find my feet in the world. I seemed to have a tendency to get into trouble but always escaped in the nick of time. I was also starting to notice that the mamby pamby girls I used to tease, make faces at, and pull their hair, seemed to have acquired certain qualities that I had not noticed before and would increasingly find attractive. I used to start to notice their legs and the two bulges in their chests; my eyes were increasingly drawn to this area. To see a glimpse of knickers under a girl's skirt reduced me to a red-faced, rosy-cheeked, brain-dead moron, without my having the least understanding of why.

To my surprise, this affliction was not confined to me alone, but also afflicted the rest of the boys. This new feeling was so powerful that we started to treat the girls differently, as if they were no longer from another planet and of no value, but a close species that we did not wish to upset, and even valued. They seemed to possess certain qualities that we wished to research further, and we knew this would not be achieved by pulling their hair and calling them names. They were no longer alien, but seemed to possess something we wanted but could not work out what this mysterious something was. We just knew we needed it, and, if we wanted it, we had to change the way we treated them.

This mysterious power the girls possessed over us was being continually refined and polished, by a flick of the hair, a wink of the eye, often coupled with a sharp movement of the lips to reveal the tongue, increasing in sophistication as the girls got older. Sometimes there was a demonstration of this power they held over us, by a flick of the skirt, revealing the flesh of their white legs, which would instantaneously turn us into Pavlov's dogs, pupils dilating, eyes wide open, looking, seeing, salivating, knowing we should be doing something, but not knowing exactly what.

We would go to any length to see a pair of knickers; my pen would have a life of its own and spend most of its time on the floor, with me bending over and picking it up. The girls were wise to this dodge at school, and knew we were up to no good. They put their hands up and said, "Please, miss, he is looking up my skirt at my knickers."

This would result in an immediate sanction and we would miss our playtime. The girls were not as stupid as we thought, but were always one step ahead, and we could never quite work out why. As a further exhibition of this power they wielded, we even let them join our gang. The younger boys thought we were going soft by allowing girls into the group, but they were not yet bewitched by this natural power we elder boys knew they possessed. Indeed, one member of our group even stated he had a girlfriend, but quickly added that kissing was not allowed. Kissing, I thought, how horrible! Most of the girls had pimples all over their faces and were forever wiping their nose.

There is no way I wanted any of this. I had pimples myself, in abundance, all over my face, and did not want anyone else's, even if they did belong to the girls. To kiss and try to avoid the spots was impossible, and kissing was definitely out, for me. There was a limit to the power of the spell they held over me, and kissing was undoubtedly a step too far. Most of the girls were always chewing gum, and to kiss one of them could result in our lips becoming stuck together. To explain this one away to my mother would be impossible. I always felt lucky, but I was far from stupid. She would have grounded me for the rest of the year, besides giving me lectures on how to be a good, clean-living boy, and I could do without this hassle, and would rather kiss my ferret than the girls.

Chapter 21

THE PIT RELIED HEAVILY upon wood to shore up the ceiling, and the saw-mill was in operation day and night. The logs had to be cut to length and transported to where they would be needed underground. Logs were delivered by the wagon load, in a never ending cycle, and tipped on the side of the mountain near the saw-mill, ready for use. Thousands of these logs lay alongside the rail track, and were stacked along the riverside, the water bank and on the mountain. The logs came in all sizes and shapes; some were neatly stacked in rows; others were just offloaded and left in large untidy heaps, and were sometimes left there for months on end, and even forgotten about for long periods, with further logs dropped on top of them, in no particular order.

The smaller logs were about two to three metres long and no more than six inches in diameter. These were scattered about everywhere and could be handled easily by one person. A lot of logs were from the pine forests of Scandinavia and Russia, and were transported over thousands of miles by rail and ship.

We were continually being warned about the dangers of the pit and ordered to keep away from the pit top. We always listened but never took any notice. The logs were always good to play in because there were so many little hiding places where we could not be seen. It was easy to build dens in the logs, and hide from the adults, especially Mr Parry, the pit policeman. We could perch on the top of the log pile and see all around us, and hide in between the log structures we had built to act as a shield from the eyes of the adults. We felt safe, little realizing the constant danger to which we were subjecting ourselves. We could only see fun.

The best dens were built out of the small, scattered logs, because they were easy to move and were always in plentiful supply. We would clear out an area in the centre of the pile and place a number of the shorter logs upright, to form a straight wall. This would be held in place by other logs, wedged across the top of the structure and held in place by cross logs, placed diagonally across the corners at various angles, to stop the inside from collapsing. Another layer of logs would be placed over the top, in the opposite direction, to further strengthen the structure, and old belting thrown over the top, to protect us against the rain. A last layer of logs would then be thrown over the construction in a random manner, to disguise the den underneath. The top would look the same as the rest of the timber yard, but the centre of the pile would be hollow, with our hideaway inside.

A passageway would be constructed from the den to the end of the pile, with the entrance facing onto the mountain. Further logs would be scattered over the entrance, for camouflage. The inside would be about three metres by two metres, and the floor would also be made of logs. There would be a sitting area, and a little table made from an old upturned bucket, together with little notches in the sides, to hold further bits and pieces.

There would be no natural light in the inner sanctuary, and we had several candles, placed in various positions around the den, and a few old coats or blankets on the floor. We were quite adept at building these constructions and could make one in a few hours. Indeed, they were often discovered and collapsed, and we would have to start to make another one, as quickly as we could. It was a constant game of cat and mouse between the pit staff and us.

Always looking for opportunities, the den offered a perfect opportunity to impress the girls. We had already accepted a few into our gang, and we told them of our den and how we take sandwiches and lemonade inside to eat. We thought we could impress them with the den, and this would allow us the opportunity to explore further the witching power they possessed. We invited a few to come and have a look inside. The best time for their visit would be after Sunday school, because they would all be wearing skirts. We reckoned that they could not get into the den without showing their knickers. That afternoon, before the girls were due to join us, a quarrel broke out as to who would go in first and who would enter the den directly after the girls. No one wished to go first, we all wanted to follow after the girls, and this almost resulted in a fight to decide the outcome. Eventually, we decided to settle it with a game of Dixie Stones.

This was a game at which I was fairly adept, and it was not long before the outcome was known - I won. Directly after the girls, I was to follow them through the tunnel and into the den. David had a torch but he would not lend it to me because he had lost the game, so I borrowed one from my house, without telling my parents, intending to have the torch back in place before they knew it had gone. What they did not know could do them no harm.

Kevin thought it unfair that I was the one to follow the girls and he started to sulk and moan about how he never wins anything, and no one cared about how he felt.

This is my gang, Kevin, and I care about how all the gang feels," I replied, seeing a way to help Kevin and help myself in the process. I knew he had six marbles, four gob stoppers and two bubble gums, as well as two coins worth four pence.

"I want you to go first, Kevin, after the girls," I said, looking at him and smiling benevolently.

His eyes lit up at this.

"Obviously, Kevin, it is only fair that you give me your marbles, gob stoppers, bubble gum and the four pence in your pocket," I added, in a quiet but caring voice.

"Can I keep the money and the marbles?" he pleaded.

I looked at him, my mouth open, eyes wide, in total surprise.

"How could you be so selfish, Kevin, after what I just offered you?" I opened my arms and showed him my approachable, honest, genuine concern about his selfish nature.

He immediately apologized. I touched him on the shoulder, to show there were no hard feelings, and he handed over all the items agreed upon. I was friendly with Pat, one of the girls, and I hoped I would get a private viewing if I shared with her half of the goodies Kevin had just given to me, except the marbles. These I would add to my collection; no amount of knickers-seeing was worth my marbles.

The girls turned up, all excited about seeing the den, but as they got closer, our faces dropped, they were all wearing trousers or shorts; there was not a skirt to be seen. They had taken these clothes to Sunday school, and changed in the toilet before meeting us. They were one step ahead of the game, again.

Kevin asked for all his things back. I pleaded that a deal is a deal and he should do the honourable thing and let me keep them. He did not feel in the least honourable and demanded all his things back immediately, or he would tell the girls what we were up to, and they would tell their mothers of our plan, and then I would be in real trouble.

Reluctantly, I handed back all the items, except the one gobstopper that I had in my mouth, secretly blaming the girls for my plight. They had never taken a change of clothes to Sunday school before, so why now? How did they know what we were planning? They approached us, smiling and laughing as if they knew of our plan, but convention would not allow them to mention the matter.

I was the first to speak.

"Welcome to our den. We have cleaned it out, because we did not want you to get your dresses dirty."

"You should have said," the girls replied in unison, all

looking innocent and coy.

One of the girls tossed her black hair back over her shoulders, slowly drew her hands over it, looked at me with a large smile on her face, and said, "You should have said, and we would not have needed to go to all this trouble and change our clothes," she said. "We only changed because we thought wearing skirts would not be right, as we are now members of the gang."

Clever, I thought. They are playing with us as they would their dolls, and I replied quickly, "Skirts are allowed, so there is no need to go to that trouble again. Feel free to just turn up."

What they were really saying was, *up yours*, we know what your game is and we are having none of it. We are more than a match for all you lot.

As a matter of fact, they were always one step ahead but would never show their hand, always playing the innocent girl routine, and we always fell for it. This spell is more powerful than I first thought.

Into the den we all went, one after the other, the order of entry did not matter now, except that the last one in had to pull a few logs over the entrance, in case the pit bobby turned up and discovered the door. The candles were lit and we talked and told stories about ghosts and ghouls, dragons and monsters, laughed and joked, while the girls pretended to be afraid.

Every few minutes, one of our gang would crawl to the entrance, pop his head up and look around, to see if the coast was still clear. Sunday always brought Mr Parry out; he knew all the dodges, and where to look for dens. If we saw him near, we had to keep quiet, or he would hear our voices, the game would be up and the den destroyed, followed by a visit to our parents. This is what we feared the most. After being so often warned about the dangers of the pit, we would be in for a rough ride if any of our parents found we were playing on its surface.

I had taken sandwiches to share with Pat but, because she was wearing trousers, I consumed them all myself. A few of the other girls asked for a bite but I refused, making the excuse that my mother would not allow it. I did share my bottle of lemonade around the group, providing someone agreed to carry the bottle afterwards, until they passed my house and had handed it back to me. Pat volunteered to do this. Secretly perhaps, she was trying to make amends for the skirt, but I shall never really know the truth.

Spring was now with us and the weather was getting warmer, which gave us the opportunity to spend more time at the den, planning how we would spend the summer and how we could avoid school. We were always fearful of adults spotting us and flattening our den, and would make doubly sure there was no one around when we entered it. This den was by far the best we had ever built and we were all immensely proud of it; it had everything we needed, and we did not want it destroyed.

We knew the pit pretty well, and the areas to avoid, and how to move around without being spotted. This particular evening, we were all coming home from the den, when I decided to stop off near the old lamp house, telling the rest to go on. There was always a lot of old lead tubes and lead radiators thrown on the floor at this spot, waiting to be thrown into a bucket for transportation to the slag heaps.

I collected some of the lead and melted it down, to make into weights and ornaments, as well as arrowheads, and I would often come here alone and raid the dump for fresh supplies. There was a lot less likelihood of me getting caught when alone, and the last thing I needed was to look after someone else, when on these lead raids.

I left the group and started down the side of the pit wall, behind Greenfield Terrace. This wall was about three to four metres in height and constructed in solid stone. I came past the two monstrosities looming up into the air, walked down behind the cleaning shed and around the corner by the pit offices, keeping close to the wall wherever possible, in order not to be spotted.

At the bottom of the pit offices, before the lamp room, was another wall, a concrete one, running down behind the lamp room, across to the baths, and ending at the back of the canteen. My eyes were watching, looking into corners and doorways, my ears listening for the sound of voices in the air, alert to any sound that was not mechanical. I had made this trip successfully many times before, and it had become a matter of routine. I knew exactly where to find the lead, and intended to fill all my pockets and a canvas bag tied around my waist, carry the lead back to the garden, and hide it under the ferret hutch until I had time to melt it down. Also at the dump were other items of value, especially the rolls of copper wire that I could use in the garden. Copper was also good to save and sell to the rag and bone man, who always paid a reasonable price, if the quantity being sold were heavy enough.

The dump was round the next corner and there was not a soul to be seen. I ran round the corner, feeling confident about not being seen, and I bumped straight into Mr Parry, hitting him full in the stomach. He grabbed me by the collar, looked down at my face and said angrily,"You are Dai's boy. What are you doing over here?"

My mind went blank and I started to stutter, not having an explanation at hand and desperately trying to think up any excuse.

"Come on, come on, what are you doing over here? I need an answer."

By this time, my whole body was shaking and the palms of my hands were starting to sweat. This meant trouble, big trouble, and I just looked at him like a frightened fox surrounded by hounds.

"Does your father know you are on the pit?" This was the third question and he was after a few answers; I must say something.

"No, sir, he does not. He is not at home, sir, and my mother is really worried. I thought he may be in the pit baths, and I was looking for someone to ask, and you are the only one I could find. I saw you walking around and thought that, if I ran after you, you might have seen him, sir." I answered politely and looked him in the eyes as I spoke, starting to find my composure.

"You come looking for me, you say?"

"Yes, sir."

To say sir, when talking to adults, makes them feel important. "I know it was wrong, Mr Parry, sir, and I have no excuse for coming on this pit. I know how dangerous it is and I can only say sorry, but I was really worried about my father. Have you seen him?" I spoke each word with concentrated concern, my composure now completely back.

"You must have known this place is out of bounds for children and it will land you in trouble. What have you got to say for yourself?" His voice was now softening.

"Nothing, Mr Parry, sir, except I love my father and would risk getting into trouble to stop my mother worrying." This was partly true; I did love my father.

"Go and see if he is in the baths, and if you get stopped, say you have my permission, but don't hang about longer than you need."

I started to run towards the baths, looked back and shouted, "Thank you, Mr Parry, sir, for being such a nice person."

I moved around the corner out of sight and into safety. I stopped, leaned against the wall and breathed a long sigh of relief. I had got out of this one by the skin of my teeth. It had definitely been a close shave, far too close for comfort. If he had caught me after I picked up the lead, it would have been the end, I would have been finished, kaput, grounded for life, but my luck held. I thanked my lucky stars.

Chapter 22

THE COLD WEATHER was still with us and, even though we covered the bottom of the doors with draft excluders, made from old nylon stocking, the legs of old trousers or any thing else we were able to make a sausage shape with, the house was always cold, unless you were sitting near the fire, and even then your back would feel cold. We used paper, rolled up into tight balls, to fill any gaps we found in the windows or walls, poking it into the small gaps with the blade of a knife. It helped but the rooms were still always cold and draughty.

Every year we moaned about these draughts, and my mother was determined to sort the problem out once and for all before next winter, and she gave her husband and everyone else that was in earshot, which meant the whole street, notice of her intention. My father shook his head, agreed totally and said that he would think about how this could be achieved; which meant nothing would be done.

A few days afterwards, my mother was talking to her brother Davy about the draughts, and he said he had recently read an article in a trade magazine about how heat always rises to the top of a room. The article said that, without insulation, most heat escapes through the ceiling and roof of the house. If the heat could be kept in the room, and not lost through the ceiling, the whole house would be warmer and cosier.

Another suggestion was to cover the inside of the windows with transparent plastic sheeting that would cling to the glass and the wood surrounds to form a tight bond, excluding all draughts. It was now Spring-time, and too late to cover the windows this year, but the loft should be insulated as soon as possible.

Mog got to hear about this and came to assess the work to be done.

"I hear you are cold, old girl."

"Don't call me old girl, Mog. It makes me feel as old as our mother," she said. Mog always called their mother the old girl, and to bestow this title on my mother was not well received.

"I may be cold, but I am not old. Be gone with you, calling me old girl."

"Ok, Lol, show me the problem."

"There is no problem, you old goat. The house is always draughty and cold, and one way to hold the warmth in, according to Davy, is to insulate the roof."

"I'll get my tools and fix it straight away."

That meant that he would go to fetch his tool kit and come back with his hammer.

My mother was aware of this and tried and put him off. "The Spring is here now, Mog, leave it for a while."

There would be no possibility of this happening. My mother used to say there was more chance of a snowball surviving in hell, than for Mog to change his mind, when he decided to do something. The only option open to my mother was to give in gracefully. If it were anyone other than Mog, she would have sent him packing straight away, but Mog held a certain place in her heart, and she would rather cut her finger off than upset her brother.

"We need insulation in the roof, to protect against the cold. You will not need tools for that," she replied, giving it one last shot.

"They will always come in handy. You never know when a hammer and a few nails are needed. I will pop over the road and be back in a few minutes."

He went marching out of the door before there was a chance to say anything. My mother might as well have kept her mouth firmly shut. She already knew this, and told me, "There will be green snow before Mog will take any notice."

But it would never stop her from trying, and at times, Mog could be *very trying,* but she loved him dearly, and that overcame all resistance, at least for the present.

A few minutes later, he was back, the trusted hammer in his hand, together with a drill and bit, a measuring tape, and a torch for light when in the attic.

"We need the insulation first," my mother insisted.

"All in good time. We need to measure the area first, and decide how we are to lay the material," he said, looking at his hammer.

My mother was now very nervous about the whole project, but did not say anything; even if she had done, it would have been to no avail.

A stepladder was taken from under the stairs and leaned against the wall at the top of the stairs. Mog climbed up and removed the attic hatch cover, and my mother handed him the torch before he climbed through into the attic. He was up in the roof, muttering and spluttering about how dirty the attic is, with the accumulated dust of years.

"This needs a good cleaning, Lol. Hand me a brush and a bag and I will clean it up."

"Leave it, Mog. Just measure the area and come down," she implored, handing up the tape measure through trap doorway. "Please come down. We can measure the area from the floor," she pleaded. "You will be careful, Mog, the ceiling is years old and not very strong," she shouted, as the sound of his feet could be heard on the rafters above. "Come down and wait for Dai to help you. He will be here shortly."

"The dust is so thick up here, I am unable to see. You need a new ceiling, not insulation. The rafters are rotten in places."

"The house does not seem as draughty as it used to be. You can come down now, Mog. I think I will leave the insulation," she said, in a last desperate attempt to get him out of the attic.

Before my mother had a chance to finish the sentence, Mog was down, but not in the manner my mother expected. He was leaning over to measure the length of the attic, when his foot got caught on one of the cross beams, he lost his balance and fell. The whole attic shook, and, in the next instant, the ceiling, with Mog closely following, came crashing down into the bedroom. Dust was everywhere, the bed was covered and Mog lay sprawled on the floor, and my mother for once lost for words.

"Mog, Mog, are you alright?" she shouted, after the shock had subsided. He looked up at her, totally covered in dirt, flat cap still on his head, and the torch still in his hand. The whole room was covered with the dust, and plaster that had remained in the ceiling for decades was now on the floor, over all the furniture and bed, and dust swirled around the room. Mog was as black as if he had just finished a shift in the pit. The room was a total wreck.

"Light us a fag, Lol," Mog said, staring up at the hole is the ceiling. "Lucky I went up there. I said the ceiling was rotten. It could have come down on your head anytime." He accepted the lit cigarette from my mother.

"What do you mean, could have come down on my head? It did come down on my head, you old goat, and all over the room," she said sarcastically, staring at Mog, who was calmly smoking his cigarette.

"It looks as if the job is going to be bigger than we originally thought, but it will be easier to insulate the ceiling now," he said, pointing to where the ceiling had been.

"What ceiling? There is no ceiling to insulate. Most of it is on the floor, with you on top," she snapped.

Sharpness and sarcasm were totally lost on Mog. There would be more understanding from the cat, but it had vanished before Mog went into the attic. Cats have a sixth sense, and it was obviously right on this occasion.

My mother started to assess the amount of work that would

need to be done to tidy the room, and she was not amused in the least. At that moment, my father walked in, took one look at the mess, at Mog, who was still sitting on the floor, and asked the obvious. "Where is the ceiling, Reen?"

The response was instant. "Where the bloody hell do you think? It is under Mog, on the floor."

My father lit his pipe, thought for a moment and then said to Mog, "You look as if you could do with a pint. Come on, let's go down the pub, to think things through while the mess is being cleaned up."

He looked at my mother as if to say, what are you hanging about for? Clean the place up. My mother instantly turned, anger spitting out of her eyes, into a dragon. This last remark was what broke the camel's back. She had had enough, and had no intention of cleaning any mess.

"Now listen here, you pair of scotch brained onions, if you think I am going to clean up this mess when you two are down the pub, swigging ale, think again, and don't give me all this planning baloney, or I will knock your two empty, bloody heads together, to try and make one brain, even though I suspect it would be no bigger than a soaked pea."

This was fighting talk from the dragon and caught the two men on the hop. They looked at my mother without saying a word. They were in deep enough already and knew when to keep their mouths firmly shut. My mother placed both arms on her hips, stamped the floor in anger as the dust firmly shot away from under her feet and created a cloud around her. She hissed at the pair, "This is your mess; do you hear me?" They both nodded their heads like two nodding dogs, acknowledging that they had heard the remark and were not about to argue. "You clean it, and I want it done now, and that means straight away, not after a pint." With that, she stomped downstairs.

My father sat on the side of the bed, emptied out his pipe on the floor, shook his head and muttered, "The ceiling needed replacing."

Mog, still on the floor, nodded in agreement.

"If we are scotched brained onions, her brain is definitely pickled in sour vinegar," my father added.

Mog said, "If she was pickled, she would turn the vinegar sour."

They both chuckled, Mog rose from the floor and they sat on the bed together, still laughing loudly.

"Women are difficult creatures. We know this from old, Dai," Mog added, lighting another cigarette to the sound of my mother clanging pots downstairs and shouting to ask if the clean up had started. "Shall we volunteer to clean up the mess?" Mog suggested.

"We might as well save the wife from doing the work," my father said, as if there were any choice. The clean-up was started and the rest of the ceiling taken down, to be replaced and insulated. The work took almost the whole day to complete. Both men worked full out, moaning periodically about the unfairness and unreasonableness of women. Unreasonable or not, they dared not go downstairs until the work was complete. They threw waste lathes and old plaster out of the window rather than face my mother when she was in this mood. The noise from downstairs equalled all the banging and commotion upstairs. She was on the warpath and her war cries left the pair in no doubt that the war was very much alive.

The following day, plasterboard was purchased and nailed to the new cross boards in the ceiling. Mog used his hammer and his nails, after all. Insulation was bought from the ironmongers and placed over the top of the plasterboard, and the room side was Artexed and painted with white emulsion. With the job completed, they went to the pub. My mother never again complained about the draught in the house, or said a word about anything to do with insulation; indeed, she was on her guard about complaining about any task to do with the house, in case Mog turned up with his hammer.

Chapter 23

THE BUDS OF THE TREES were showing, grass had started to grow again, the garden planting had been completed. The tender plants were under glass, waiting to be planted out after the threat of frost had gone. The weather was still cold in the mornings, but the days were pleasant. There was that expectation in the air that we all experience when spring breaks and summer is just around the corner.

The den had still not been discovered and we were looking forward to the warm summer days. We hoped to invite the girls to join us as part of the gang. After the last episode, they had not been back to the den, because the weather had been too cold, but now that summer was coming, there could be no excuse. A little way up from the den and across the valley, before the start of the pit, was the river. Every summer, we made a dam with stones and clods from the banks. This created a pool large enough to play, swim and have fun in, especially, we thought, this year, with the girls.

We started by carrying large stones from the riverbed and placing them in a line across the river, to form the first barrier against the water. Another row was placed about a half a metre below, and the inside filled with small stones and clods, rammed down with the logs we took from the pit. A channel was made in the centre of the construction, to allow the water an outlet. After a few days, the pool was complete.

We met that evening at the den, and Brian outlined a cunning plan about how we could watch the girls changing into their bathing costumes without them knowing that we were up to no good.

"You all know that I am a hunter and a stalker, and these skills I will share with you."

When Deadeye talked in this way, we knew he was after something, and would normally give him a wide berth. His plans always landed us in trouble, so we quickly said, "No," adding sharply that we had no sweets and no money and did not wish to go hunting on his terms. He assured us that the plan would work and there was no catch to the idea. We agreed to listen, without committing ourselves, because if there was any way we could watch the girls undressing, we were interested.

The plan was cunningly simple. We would build the girls their very own changing area, so they could change in private and not worry about anyone seeing them. Kevin thought for a moment – he was always quick off the mark, and said, "Yes, I see the plan. We will knock it down before they can use it, so we can watch them changing."

"What good is that, Kev? Why build it in the first place?" I asked.

"I never thought of that."

I thought to myself, Einstein would never die as long as Kevin was alive, but did not tell him so, in case he got carried away and decided to become an ideas man.

The further up the river you travelled, the larger the rocks that protruded from the mountain side, next to where the river flowed down the valley. The water was continually eroding the banks and exposing large rocks on both sides. At one spot, two of these large stones stood together, side by side, and narrowing, until they came together at one end.

"This is the ideal spot to supply the girls with their very own changing area," Deadeye remarked.

We placed a few logs over the top of the two large rocks, threw belting over the entrance and the top, to make a doorway, and placed a round stone and a flat piece of wood into the construction, for the girls to sit on when changing. The trap was set; now all we needed was the bait. They would have to be smart to get round this one, we all thought.

The plan seemed to be deadly effective. The sides of the two rocks that came together had an area behind large enough for a few people to hide at the back, so, provided we kept quiet, there was no chance of discovery. We could enter this gap from the top, and not be seen from the front. There was no way the girls would know we were behind the two stones. The plan was foolproof and we congratulated ourselves, believing the girls would be no match for us this time. Minxes they may be, but we were foxes, more cunning and devious.

To be extra careful, we even pushed a hollow drainpipe through the only gap between the two stones, to form a spy hole at the top of the structure, and placed a small mirror angled into the changing area, in order to look through the tube above their heads. This meant we would not be looking directly at them changing, and they would be unable to see us. There was no way we could be discovered. There was not the slightest doubt in our minds that they would fall for our plan. There was no way out of this one, we felt, and victory was near.

"When shall we tell the girls of the plan," Kevin asked.

"We don't ever tell them, Kev; that is the whole point," Gerald explained, wondering why he bothered. "If they know we are looking at them changing, they will tell their parents, they would tell ours, and we would be for it."

When common sense was handed out, Kevin was not just behind the door but totally off the planet. I reckon that when he was born, his mother had him delivered standing up, and when he dropped out, he landed on his head, knocking all sense back into his mother's stomach, because it definitely did not stay with him.

"What if the girls ask where we are changing?" Kevin asked.

"That is a good point. They may get suspicious if there is no area for us," Gerald commented, and we all looked at Kev.

Maybe he was more intelligent than we gave him the credit for. We were all astounded at an original thought emanating from the mouth of our friend.

"What is your plan, Kev," I asked, thinking there must be some intelligence there after all.

Kev looked around blankly, his eyes expressionless, as if he had been asked to invent the wheel. He thought for a moment, another rare occurrence with Kev, his eyes lit up, and he said, "I know; we all change together."

We shook our heads in disbelief. It was the general consensus that he had swallowed a large quantity of *twp pills,* to help the brain cells in his feet that were obviously suffering from a serious foot ache.

"This is a secret plan. The girls will not wish to change with us, Kev. We want to see them changing without them knowing," Gerald said, making the point again but realizing that the paper was blank and there would be difficulty in making the writing stick.

"He has a point, if you think about it," Deadeye remarked.

This is too much to take in, I thought, Deadeye is now thinking and asking us to think about what Kevin just said. The plan is not going well. We are putting too much brainpower into the project.

"The point, I mean, about our own changing area, not for the girls to suspect anything," he quickly added, not to stay too long with Kevin's line of thinking, in case the rest of us thought he was also a secret *twp pill* addict.

It was generally agreed that we build our own changing area, and we constructed it from a few logs collected from the pit, set around one of the trees overhanging the riverbank. This construction did not take long because none of us would be using it, anyway. We picked the most secluded area, because we could always tell the girls we were changing in our area, when we would have been spying on them.

The pond was now complete. The weather was getting warmer and as the weekend approached, we persuaded the girls to come and have a swim on the Saturday morning. It was a tradition for gang members to go swimming as early in the year as possible, or so we led them to believe. We made a big show about how we valued their company and appreciated their friendship, and went on about the way we had built them a changing area as a sign of respect, to allow them to change into their bathing costumes in private. They agreed to bring sandwiches and lemonade to share with us, as a sign of us being all good friends and firm members of the gang, and we agreed to build a large fire on the bank, to keep them warm after their swim. I collected a pile of wood and ferns from the surrounding mountain and made the fire. This time, we thought, this time, they will not outsmart us this time.

We called for the girls on Saturday morning, assuring their mothers that we would look after them and not go near the pit. We all met beforehand and warned Kevin not to have any brilliant ideas and to not mention anything about our plan. We recognized that Kevin was the weak link, and we were not going to take any chances in this area. Wherever possible, we were to keep him away from the girls. The lot of us walked together towards the pond, laughing and joking and generally enjoying each other's company in a light-hearted spirit of friendship and fun.

"We know something you don't know." Kevin announced, smiling and laughing, and then placing both hands over his mouth, as if to stop a secret from falling out by accident. We all became aware that the falling out was a real possibility and were on tenterhooks. Gerald gave him help to keep the secret in, by placing his hands over Kev's mouth. To be extra careful, we also sent him on ahead as a scout, well away from the girls.

We arrived at the river bank and laid out a base camp, placing all our sandwiches and drinks in the centre, and settled down for a while, talking and laughing, sitting on our towels and the ground sheets we had brought for the occasion. A few of the girls went paddling in the cold water and came running back every few minutes, avoiding the stinging nettles, to warm their feet at the fire, which was now fully alight and glowing red.

Deadeye was the first to propose that we all change into our bathing trunks, and suggested to the girls that they may wish to do the same. David said he would show them their very own changing area, and went into detail about all the trouble we had put into the construction, to save their modesty. The girls followed David to their changing area, while Gerald kept Kevin at bay. A few of the boys ran around to the spy hole, ready for the fashion show.

The girls all returned and said how grateful they were for our thoughtfulness, and thanked us for our trouble.

"It was no trouble, honestly," I said impatiently, but trying to cover the anger and frustration in my voice. "It is the least we can do. Now, go and get changed into your bathing costumes. The water is really clear and inviting, so hurry up," I urged.

Elaine asked the whereabouts of our changing area.

"We have just a small area around that tree." I pointed to the tree in the distance. "Our changing area is tiny and a lot further to walk, so go and get changed. We are all waiting to go into the water."

The girls would not be rushed; they asked to see our changing area and then said they would go and get changed. This is the last hurdle, I thought. We had been planning this for weeks, so a few more minutes would make no difference. I agreed to show them our changing area.

This bore no comparison to theirs, and I thought there would be no problem here. Besides, it was a decent way from the river, in a damp, secluded corner, under a tree. The only reason we built the construction was as a decoy, not to make the girls suspicious. They all looked at the changing area, looked back at us, and Christine said, "We will change here. This spot will do for us."

"No, no," I replied, "this is our area, it is not good enough for you girls."

Pat answered, "All the trouble you boys have been to in constructing our changing area shows how you respect us, and we feel so honoured, so much so, in fact, that we decided to give you a surprise and let you use the best changing area. We will use this one instead."

This could not be happening, I thought.

"Please, please, we want you to have the other changing area. That is why we built it for you," I insisted, trying to get them to reconsider.

"No," Pat said forcefully. "This is the least we can do after all your trouble, and furthermore, we have all brought welsh cakes and sweets to share with you, as a further gesture of friendship."

You could have knocked me over with a spoon. What could I say? We needed neither welsh cakes nor sweets, we just needed the girls to change where they were told to, and not to make up their own minds and use our changing area.

"There are grass snakes around this area. I saw one only a few minutes ago; they are dangerous and may frighten you, so use the other changing area." I said, in one last desperate attempt to get them to change their minds.

"Where, where, is the snake?" one of the girls shouted.

We are making progress, I thought, adding quickly, "There may be more than one. I have heard this is a breeding area for baby snakes. So don't change here."

"No, no," two of the girls screamed, "We both like snakes and we would like to see a few. Where did you see them? Tell us, so we can look. We will definitely change here now, and hope we may be able to see a few."

We were beaten good and proper; the girls had their way, and changed where we were unable to see them, our carefully laid plan again in tatters.

The girls, in full bathing costumes, joined us in the pool a little later and we all had a good afternoon, splashing about in the cold water, running back to the fire and back to the water again, enjoying each other's company. We lost Kevin for a while and, when we found him, we asked where he had been.

"Watching at the changing area," he beamed.

"But why, Kev? The girls are not using it," Gerald remarked.

"No one told me," he replied.

"Kev, the girls have already changed, been in the water and changed back again and gone home. They were in the water the same time as you."

"I did not think," he replied, thought for a moment and then added; "That is why I did not see them in the changing hole."

He was happy that he had now solved the problem. We all looked at each other. What more could we say, other than, "Have a sweet, Kev."

"He is brain dead," Deadeye remarked, and off home we all trotted, outwitted by the girls again.

Chapter 24

ESPITE ALL THE DUST and dirt from the pit, there was a
fierce pride in the way the women kept their houses
clean. There were exceptions to this rule, but, generally,
the standard of cleanliness and tidiness was high. It was their way
of fighting back; the home was their haven and retreat, and there
was a pride in how the house was kept clean, including the front
step, even on some occasions to excess. They did not have
much, but what they did have would be kept clean.

Our next door neighbour directly up from us was one such
person, a dear old lady whom we knew as Mrs. Evans three
hundred, to differentiate her from all the other Evanses, and
there were a few around at that time. Three hundred was the
number of the house she shared with her son. Mrs. Evans was
forever cleaning the house, and the front step would be brushed
first thing in the morning, before lunch, after lunch, and, once
more for luck, in the late afternoon. The only time I can
remember the front step having a rest from this constant
brushing was on Christmas Day and I suspect it was swept then,
too, but I was not aware of it.

Her carpets suffered the same fate, hung on the clothesline in
the back yard, and bashed in the morning, bashed in the
afternoon, bashed in the evening. After each bashing, the carpets
would be removed, placed back on the floor and the whole floor
covered in newspaper, to keep the carpets clean. Every time I
went into Mrs. Evans' house, I was not allowed to walk on the
carpets, only the paper, which was easy because the whole floor
and the table were covered with old newspapers. The
newspapers served as a paper table cloth and were changed after

every meal. She collected all the old newspapers from the local newsagent, old man Chislet, and opened them up to cover the house.

I could never quite work out why the carpets were bashed so much and placed back on the floor; perhaps she was a secret carpet hater, and needed to extract revenge every day, and then cover the evidence of these bashings and beatings with paper. For all this bashing, Mrs. Evans was a true lady, always ready to help, and would not, or could not, say a bad word about anyone. Whenever I went into the house, there was always something to eat and drink. She was a very private lady and did not follow the normal tradition of roaming other houses and allowing people to roam her house. The only time you entered her house was by invitation. She was well educated and knew about books: Shakespeare, Jane Austen, and a lot more that we did not know, but she would never mention any of them, unless asked to do so.

Her door was always on the latch, for all of her private ways. Locking doors was not something the older people believed in. Her door would always be open, like the doors of most of the old valley people. There was a code of trust and this trust was very rarely abused. To enter a house and steal was almost inconceivable to the old Rhondda people. They believed in sharing, they were as one, behaved as one, shared as one, and you do not rob from yourself. How can you?

All the old people remembered the real hardships of the valley, the constant lockouts and the frequent strikes that were common between the Two World Wars. If they had it, they would share it, and you would have it, so why steal it?

These real hardships were etched into the memory of the old people. The long strikes, the constant struggle to eat, the scavenging for coal from the slag heaps to keep warm, when the pit Barons tried to starve them and break their spirits in time of conflict, because they would not work longer and harder for less wages, and do what they were told in order to make more profit.

The reminders of this time can still be seen all over the valley. The old slag heap at the top of our street we termed the humps, on account of all the craters and holes dug into the surface, a constant reminder of how the old miners scavenged for coal in the long strike of 1926, a strike that lasted over a year. The Barons called it a strike; my father termed it a lock-out, which would be nearer the mark. The men were locked out because they dared to challenge and question the power of Black Gold.

These holes were found all over the old slag heaps, made by hungry miners, in order to have heat in the houses and fuel to cook the food grown in the vegetable plot that kept them alive. This was a time when *valley pride* was at its height, and they were truly as one, bonded together, helping, supporting, and encouraging each other, as only a close knit mining community would know how.

Next down from our house lived another old lady; there always seemed to be lots of old ladies, their husbands long dead, destroyed by the pit, the breath choked out of them by the same dust that strangled my grandfather, and looked on by the mine owners as dispensable casualties, no more than a price that must be paid.

Mrs. Chamberlain was in our house frequently and was always good for a few sweets and the occasional jam sandwich. Solid and proud, not particularly educated like Mrs. Evans, but as sharp as a Comanche's knife, if she thought you were trying to pull a fast one. My mother and she used to be very friendly, and were often sitting in our house, talking, when I came home from school. There was many a time when I thought Mrs. Chamberlain lent my mother the Comanche knife, because she would try to skin me alive if she caught me up to no good, which used to happen with increasing regularity as I got older.

Chapter 25

WE DID NOT GIVE UP on the girls; another plan needed to be worked out; we could not let them outsmart us all the time. At the den that night, we held a secret planning session on how we are to approach this problem.

"Why don't we just ask to see their knickers?" Kevin asked.

"They won't agree to that, Kev. They would know what we are up to and then there is no way our plan will work," David replied.

"Why don't we play soldiers up the Target, and when we shoot them and they roll down dead, we are bound to see their underclothes? This plan cannot fail," Gerald remarked.

We all looked at each other, thought for a moment and David said reflectively, "This may work; they cannot be that smart?"

The Target was a flat area of mountain above Vicarage Terrace, extending down to my grandmother's house at the top end of Chepstow Road. Part of this mountain was planted with conifer trees and owned by the Forestry Commission, areas of which were out of bounds. If the adults could not keep us off the pit, there was no chance that the forestry workers could stop us roaming where we wished.

The plan was to invite the girls for a picnic and, after the picnic, to play soldiers. They would shoot at us first; we would fall down and pretend to be shot; and then it would be their turn. The best one to fall and pretend to die would be the winner. They would not think to wear trousers, we thought, because they would wish to look nice for the picnic.

The day arrived and up the Target Mountain we all went. The plan was working; they were all dressed in skirts, and dressed up for the afternoon picnic. This is it, we thought.

"Take it slow," whispered Deadeye, portraying his hunting skills.

We sat on the grass and laid out a blanket on the ground, placed the food and drink for the picnic on the top, laughing and joking with each other, and I suggested a game of drop dead. All the boys readily agreed, having eating the food on the blanket, and we went first, running and falling all over the place, as the girls pretended to shoot us. The girls would choose the best drop-dead act and we would then do the same for them, or so we thought.

The girls were enjoying the fun and shot us, using sticks from the nearby trees as guns. We were falling all over the place, laughing, joking, shouting and showing off generally, trying to impress the girls with our drop down dead acting skills. We then suggested changing over, and we shoot at them and they pretend to drop down dead. They eagerly agreed to change sides and participate in the game, and I said that we would choose the best drop-dead winner.

We were just about to change over sides, when we heard adults speaking and walking toward us. You could have knocked us down with a feather. Standing before us were the parents of Pat and Elaine, out walking. They approached us and sat on the floor to rest, asked us how the picnic went and what games we were playing.

"Drop down and die games," Gerald replied.

"Pity the girls did not know about this game before the picnic as they would not have worn their best frocks. Shall I go home, Pat, and get your trousers, and call in for the rest of you girls, and ask your parents for a change of clothes?" Pat's father asked, eager to be of service.

Foiled again, I thought, that is the last time. No more planning; from now on, I will stick to playing marbles and football. The girls had outfoxed us again. We later found out that they had asked their parents to fetch them at this time. I suspect they did not trust our intentions and the girls were right. This would be the last trick we would play on the girls; they were too clever for us. We thought we were too clever for them, and they allowed us our little game, knowing we would not succeed.

The girls went home with their parents and we were left to our own devices. The game held no attraction for us any more, so we all sat down on the grass to rest.

"We will not need these again," Deadeye said, throwing the sticks away and lying back on the grass.

"I am sticking to my ferret from now on," I remarked.

"Girls cannot be trusted to do what we want," David said ruefully."

"They are very deceitful, to play this trick on us and ask their parents to come and collect them. I don't trust them any more. They have had their last chance," Deadeye said with a sigh.

"They will never make boys," Kevin stated with certainty.

We looked at Kevin when he made this remark.

"We all know they will never make boys, Kev. Tell us something we do not know," we all shouted in unison.

He smiled, looked at us all and said, "I thought our plan may not work, so I brought these, so that you can all see what knickers look like." He delved into his rucksack and pulled out a pair of his mother's white knickers. Holding them up in the air and smiling, he placed one of the legs over his head.

"Where did you get them from, Kev?" David asked.

"Off my mother's washing line," he replied.

We all started to laugh.

"The whole point is to see them on the girls, not on your head, you jam doughnut," Gerald said, still laughing.

"There is more brain in an ounce of salt," David told Kev. "In one grain."

"I'm right, he is brain dead."

Deadeye stood up and stared at Kevin, who looked ridiculous

with the knickers still over his head, but thinking he was doing us a favour. We all loved him really. No one could dislike Kevin. The girls thought he was wonderful, despite his kokum ways. His demeanour was always cheerful, and when Kevin was around, there was never a dull moment.

"Come on, Kev, let's go home," I said, and we started to walk down off the Target.

Chapter 26

"THERE WILL BE A GOOD CROP this year, the runner beans will be exceptional," said my father, when we were on our knees in the garden, weeding in between the carrot beds. Fresh runner beans, straight from the garden, cut into pieces, cooked, and served with a dollop of butter and fresh bread make me squeak with delight, even now. The taste and smell of the tender, fresh, organic vegetable are indescribably delicious.

One of our heifers was about to give birth to a calf. It was now several months since my father had called the vet, old man Capron, who had artificially inseminated the animal. She was overdue by a few days, and we were getting concerned about the situation. The vet was called in and he decided to leave things for a few days to see if calf would be born naturally. Another week passed, and still we were waiting. The mother was now exceptionally large, and we called the vet again. This time, he was worried and informed us that a caesarean operation might be necessary because it looked as if the calf was too large to pass through the animal's pelvic bone.

This was a tricky operation and could result in the loss of the calf and its mother. The operation was planned for the next day, if nothing happened in the meantime, and we were advised to have on hand plenty of hot water and clean rags. The operation would be performed in the cowshed, and we had to make sure the floor was washed, scrubbed and disinfected that morning.

Just after lunch the following day, all was ready and we were waiting and ready for the vet. There was no sign of the calf being born naturally, and the heifer was already showing increased signs of severe stress and discomfort. We knew something had to be done quickly, or mother and calf would die.

The vet arrived as planned; the heifer was already in the cowshed, tethered to the front, standing on its feet, in obvious distress and discomfort, awaiting developments. I was to be on standby, should more hot water be called for, and my father was to help with the operation. Not long before we were due to start, Mog turned up to see if he could be of any help. He had a sixth sense and would turn up whenever there was something out of the ordinary happening. On this occasion, he was more than welcome, if only to give moral support.

"Show me what I need to do, Dai. I am at your disposal."

"Everything is under control, Mog. The operation is about to commence; we can manage; there is no problem."

"Ok, you need me on standby. Where shall I stand? We could loosen the calf by squeezing the stomach. Come, I'll squeeze this side and you two the other," he said, starting to move nearer the animal.

"No, no," the vet countered sharply. "You cannot squeeze the calf out as if you were squeezing a tube of toothpaste."

"Why don't we try and wind the animal by placing it against the side wall and running at it? If we can wind her, perhaps she would shit the calf out. What do you say, Dai," he asked, looking at my father and ignoring the vet.

"I think we should do as the vet suggested, and help with the operation. Hammering the calf out by winding its mother is not the answer, Mog."

"You may have a point. OK, when do we start?" he asked, as he rolled up his sleeves and lit another cigarette.

I had visions of my uncle chiselling at the back end of the animal, to widen the pelvic bone, hammer in hand, singing; "Hi Ho, Hi Ho and out the calf will go." We all looked at him, wondering what he would suggest next. Mog was in full swing and past the point of reasoning. He needed to do something, whatever something was, so my father asked him to hold the animal's head and stroke its face and nose.

The creature was given an injection in the side of its neck, and the side of its stomach was shaved. Watching the vet at work intrigued me totally. Within a short time, the calf could be seen, attached to the cow, as it was pulled out by my father and the vet. Mog stretched his neck to see what was going on, more concerned with the operation than the cow's head.

"Marvellous, marvellous. It's a bull calf." Mog announced, showing that he was aware of what was going on.

The calf was alive. It was taken to a corner of the cowshed and cleaned and dried with the rags provided for the purpose. It looked so helpless, lying on the floor, unable to move, as it drew its first breaths. The vet started to stitch up the cow, happy that the job was almost over and both animals were going to survive.

Next, the vet went over to check the calf and ascertain the level of stress it was experiencing after the operation, which seemed to be minimal.

"Well, Dai, the operation is a success. Watch the mother for a few days, especially over the next twenty-four hours, as the anaesthetic wears off. I'll be back in about a week, to take out the stitches, but if there are any problems, call me immediately." The vet cleaned his hands and removed his overalls.

My father brought the calf round for the mother to see, and placed it on the floor directly in front of her. The cow started to lick her calf and it responded. The only task left for me to perform was to clean up the floor with disinfected water, lay fresh bedding for mother and son, top up the water trough with fresh water, and fill the manger with hay. A quick brush under the cow and around the pen took a few minutes, and the floor was ready to cover with clean, new bedding.

I started to spread the straw and sawdust on the floor, and then it happened. The cow gave a mighty moo as all the gas in its stomach was released in one mighty movement. It came with the force and speed of a bullet. I was standing right behind the animal, busying myself with the bedding, and I was covered in manure, all over my neck, face, hair and head, followed by an immediate whoosh of urine, to wash the lot down over the rest of me.

I staggered backwards until my back fell against the far wall of the shed, wet, smelly, disgustingly dirty, as the foul stench dripped off me, Mog rushed up with rags and started to wipe me down, while I fought back tears.

"It could be worse; you could have swallowed some of it."

"I have swallowed a lot of it. My mouth was open," I answered between sobs. "It tastes horrible. I want to go home."

"Don't go home like that. Wash the worst off in the stream first," my father said, trying to show sympathy and hold his smile at the same time.

"This is not funny, you know. I could have choked," I shouted.

The men could hold back no longer, and burst out laughing. I was in the corner, feeling totally dejected and humiliated by the action of the cow. I was sure the cow had been talking to our cat in secret, and they both hatched a plot to get back at me for what I did on New Year's Eve. They definitely succeeded with a vengeance. I knew exactly how the cat felt, but with a lot more poured over me than I had poured over the cat. What a rotten cow she was, to do this to me. I was sure our cat was around somewhere, looking on and laughing with double vengeance at my ridiculous predicament.

My mother was not amused with the way I looked or smelt, but she knew it was not my fault. I had had enough of the garden, and did not intend to help my father any more, but decided to spend all my time training my ferret to catch rats and to work with our dog, Russ.

Next to the shed that housed my ferret, just across the small brook from my garden was another plot, larger than the one we owned, where a long row of sheds had been built as pigpens. Vic John owned this land and was referred to as Vic the pig man, he was a blacksmith by day and a pig-keeper the rest of the time. He could be seen every Sunday with his pick-up van, collecting all organic waste from householders and shops, and from the pit canteen. All this was boiled in his pig sheds, mixed with oatmeal and fed to his pigs. As the waste was boiled, the smell would be all around the mountain and in our houses.

The boiling took place every Sunday afternoon. The stink would be pungent, and if wind happened to be blowing in your direction, you were left in no doubt the pig man was on the boil. This smell could, nevertheless, not compete with the smell that my father was able to generate, when it was time to breathe through the mouth to improve your character. Nothing could outdo that smell, which was in a league of its own. Even though not as strong and less noticeable, it was still hard on the nose and, at close quarters, could be quite repugnant.

Sunday afternoon was also the time when the sties had their weekly clean out. The waste from the pigpens would be barrowed to the end of the garden and thrown into the brook that ran alongside the garden. Over the years, this waste had built up by the side of the brook, and now formed part of the riverbank.

It became a haven for rats, and was covered in their burrows. These rats could be quite hefty, and they were always in our garden, in the chicken sheds, and around the brook, at sunset, scavenging for food. There were several cats kept around the pig sheds and in our garden, to help to keep the rats at bay, but they were frequently fighting a losing battle. The rats bred faster than the cats could catch them. We all had dogs, too, but no sooner did we destroy one batch of rats, than another lot took their place. This battle could never be won as long as pig waste was being heaped over the river banking and left to rot. It made an ideal home and breeding ground for rats, and the battle between us was never-ending.

The ferrets would go into the rat holes and drive the rats into the open, where the dogs would be waiting to catch them, toss them into the air, and kill them in the process.

We trained the dogs to not harm the ferret, and it was safe with them. We would then catch the ferret and move to the next burrow. This was a sport we enjoyed and we often spent hours with our ferrets, catching and killing rats.

Deadeye and I were now firm friends, indeed, he was my best friend, and we spent a lot of time in each other's company, with our dogs, Russ, my terrier, and Bull's-eye, Brian's corgi. We loved these dogs and they would be with us wherever we went, except to school, and if he could have got the dog into his pocket, Deadeye would have even taken his dog there. We became quite adept at finding where to place the dogs and ferrets to best advantage, and held a bit of a reputation as rat catchers. We would know where the rats came out from their burrow and would be waiting, occasionally catching the rats in nets and cages, for later sport.

Often on a Sunday evening,, when we caught a few rats, we took them in cages to the bottom end of the pit, opposite Railway Terrace, but away from the rail track that ran near the houses, and over to the far track, by the river, where we could not be seen. There was always a number of empty wagons shunted into a siding, waiting to be filled with coal from the coal hopper further up the rail track, nearer the pit. The wagons would be totally enclosed, except for the top. The sides were higher than our heads, and we would climb up and sit on the top, ready for the entertainment.

"Tip in the rats. Quick, hurry up," David urged. I was holding the cage with the rats inside and balancing on top of the wagon.

Deadeye was sitting next to me, holding the sack with the ferret inside, and looking every inch the intrepid hunter. He shouted, "Come on. I am waiting. All get up on the wagon. We are ready to start. I'll be dropping the bag in shortly. There are three rats against my polecat. How long do you think the fight will last?"

"Five minutes," I shouted, pulling a lead weight I had recently made out of my pocket to represent my bet.

"Rubbish. The polecat is huge," remonstrated Gerald. "It will be over in two, at the most."

"There are three rats and they could put up a good fight, say ten minutes," David declared.

"The fight will last for at least fifteen minutes, I bet anyone ten marbles," Deadeye declared.

He must have inside knowledge, I thought, and immediately retracted my bet and placed the lead weight back into my pocket.

"Six marbles that the rat with a bent tail will win," was Kevin's contribution to the conversation.

"We are not betting on the rat winning, Kev; why bet on the rat?" I asked.

"Because I feel like, and I like the colour of that rat," he replied.

Deadeye looked at Kevin, shook his head and said, "Kev, the rat never wins, the ferret is like the weasel and preys on rats. The rat cannot win. This is not the way nature intended. The ferret will always win."

Kevin was quiet for a few moments and then asked, "Why can't the ferret change its nature and let the rat win?"

Kevin was in his intellectual mood again, we all thought.

Deadeye said, "Hold on, Kev. I'll have a word with my polecat, to see if it will change its nature and let the rats win." He pretended to ask the polecat to be better natured.

The rats were let loose into the wagon and, a few moments later, the ferret was released. The rats fought back for a few minutes but it was not long before the superior skills of the polecat triumphed and the three rats lay dead on the floor of the wagon. The time taken was just under fifteen minutes; the exact time Deadeye had foretold. His superior hunting skills held again. I retracted my stake, just in time, I thought, as the others were handing over their bet.

"Run, quick, we have been clocked," one of the boys shouted. "Mr. Parry has spotted us."

We all looked towards the coal hopper, and there he was, walking stick in hand, waving it in the air at us and shouting, "Get off the pit. If I catch you I'll knock all your heads together."

"Quick, Brian, grab the ferret and hand it to me," I screamed, as I jumped down off the wagon, falling over in the process. I jumped up and shouted to Brian to let the ferret drop in my hands.

"Here, have it, and be quick, old Parry is catching up," Deadeye snarled, and dropped the animal into my waiting hands. I ran down the railway line, up across the banking behind Railway Terrace, to the back of the houses facing the front main road, and then through into the main street, Parc Road, with the ferret safely tucked into my coat pocket. The other boys all ran in different directions, to confuse the enemy, Mr Parry, who would never chase us when we were off the pit.

We met at the den that evening and I handed the ferret back to Deadeye. He was now inseparable from his dog; find Bull's-eye and you would find Brian, find Brian and Bull's-eye would be following. We had given up on the girls and decided dogs and ferrets were far less trouble. A few weeks ago, we had voted girls into our gang and now we decided to vote them off again.

We used different coloured marbles to cast our votes. We would follow democratic principles and tell them the vote was close, but omit to pass on the results. That way, they would not know who had voted them out of the gang. We were still not quite sure of this magic the girls held over us, and we did not wish to upset them too much, until we understood this new feeling a bit better. These feelings were increasing as time went forward, and seemed to be getting more powerful with every week that passed. The five of us voted. Red marbles signified no; green ones yes. The result was, as expected, one to five.

"There are only five of us. How come we have five no votes and one yes? The vote should be nil to five," remarked Gerald.

"I voted twice because I want to vote for them to stay and to not stay in the gang. I could not make up my mind," Kevin replied.

"You can't do that, Kev. We all decided to vote the girls off the gang. Take the green marble back" remonstrated David.

"No, I don't feel like, so there," Kevin said, and left the situation as it was: five for, one against.

"How are we going to tell the girls?" I asked.

"Straight out," Deadeye answered, ever the diplomat.

"I'm going to tell them I voted for them to stay in the gang," Kevin stated, a large smile on his face.

"You tell them, David," Gerald spluttered, looking at him as he spoke.

"No way. Tell them yourself," David replied.

"Some one must tell them; we could do it all together," I proposed.

"That is a good idea. You go first," Kevin said, face now beaming.

"If I go first, Kev, we won't be doing it all together," I replied.

It was obvious that no one wished to tell the girls they were no longer members of the gang.

"They must be told," Deadeye shouted.

"You must tell them then," I shouted back.

"No way, no way. I am a hunter, not a girl charmer," he insisted.

What this had to do with the conversation I do not know, but

I was not about to ask, in case the rest of them volunteered me for the task.

"I know, I have it," Kevin said, clearly now in the driving seat and getting more confident with every word. "We will keep it a secret and not tell them. They think they are still in the gang, but we will know different."

This seemed a brilliant idea and we unanimously agreed that the girls had been expelled from the gang but we were not going to tell them.

Chapter 27

A FEW DAYS LATER, I had been home from school about twenty minutes when a loud sound was heard from the pit; not the usual siren signalling the end and start of the next shift, but a long, loud, shrieking, continual noise that filled the whole valley. The women knew this sound; it is the death sound screaming into the air, filling the ears with uncertainty. There had been an accident underground; this meant one, or maybe several, of their loved ones had been injured or killed. This sound renders the women immobile, frozen in time for a split moment. Fear sped like lightening across the valley, as if laughing at the people frozen with fright. Black Gold was having fun today, toying with its pawns as the rest of the valley stood waiting, fearing the worst.

The accident happened on the afternoon shift. The women would have already known the shift their husbands were working. Women whose men were working the day or night shift would breathe a sigh of relief, knowing the death knock was not to be for them this time. The rest would be in sudden shock. Their loved one was under the ground: father, husband, or son. Fearing the worst, there was panic as the women dropped everything and ran to the pit, shaking with fright. A look of shock and horror was on their faces as they stood at the pit entrance, hoping, pleading for information and praying that it would be someone else's man, not theirs.

A quiet calm descended over the crowd, all too shocked to shout and make a noise as the clouds of trouble congregated over their heads. Fear had them in its grip. No one spoke; hands covered faces. The men were due to arrive now, to go down into the death hole to mount a rescue, giving no thought for their own safety, ready to risk all for one of their own. The older miners had done this before and knew the dangers. The rescue service arrived. No one yet knew the scale of the fall underground, but the first indications were bad. A number of people had been working on the coal seam when the roof gave way, trapping the men beneath and behind the fall.

The first fears were well-founded. There had been an explosion and the roof-fall had trapped at least fifteen people. The roof-fall had been on the left wing tunnel, trapping a number of men behind. No one yet was sure if they were still alive. A large section of the roof had caved in and was covering the whole front end of the tunnel for a length of at least twenty metres. There was also a risk of gas in the tunnel, and a risk of fire, which delayed a rescue attempt until the area had been rendered safe.

Gas and foul air are constant dangers underground, and accounted for most of the explosions and roof falls. They say that this is what happened with this roof fall: gas had built up and exploded.

No one yet knew who the trapped miners were, and everyone was afraid to speculate. Philip John pushed past, shouting that his son Dennis worked the left wing. Philip wanted to know where he was and if he was all right. Mog was now part of the crowd. He was walking over to the baths, to change and go underground, to help in the rescue, if needed. "What shift is your lad working, PJ?" Mog asked.

"This shift, Mog. He works the left wing. Have you heard any news?"

Mog could see PJ was frantic with worry and tried to alleviate his concern. "Things will be alright, PJ. Your son is sharp and will know what to do in danger. You wait; he will be up shortly." Mog told him, placing his hand on his shoulder.

"I feel bad, Mog; thing are not right. Oh, God! Oh God! I

feel sure my son is gone. Please say I am wrong, please, Mog, say things are alright," he stammered, tears in his eyes, his lips trembling. "What do I tell my wife? Oh, Mog, what can I do? He is our only son. We waited five years for our Dennis. What do I tell his mother?" Mog, for once, was lost for words, a rare occurrence for him. He just looked at PJ, turned away and looked at the floor.

"How can I face my Joan? This will finish her; she has not been well for months."

Mog tapped him on the shoulder and said, "Look, old boy, let us find out, one way or another. I think things might be alright. You could be worrying unnecessarily. Just you wait and see." Mog tried to comfort him, but, secretly, he feared the worst and was unable to look PJ in the eyes. Mog stood beside PJ, who was leaning against the wall of the baths for support. "Sit on the step and have a cigarette."

PJ took a cigarette from Mog but his hands were shaking uncontrollably and he could not light it before the match went out. Mog lit another cigarette and handed it to PJ. He placed it to his lips and drew the smoke greedily into his lungs, as if he were trying to inhale and send the smoke deep into the ground, to act as a hand to drag his son up to the safety of the pit top. He held the smoke for a few seconds, and forcefully exhaled, as if trying to spew his son out of his mouth and into the light and his open arms.

"He is alright. Tell me, Mog, everything is OK."

Mog could not do it; he just placed his hand on PJ, as they sat by the wall, without speaking another word.

Other people were now arriving, concerned and worried but, as yet, no news was forthcoming; the only thing to do was to wait. The rescue service was keeping everyone back until a full assessment from their colleagues already underground was received on the surface, detailing the extent of the problems and what further dangers could be identified.

For the people on the surface, the wait seemed endless, not knowing, counting every second, as the time slowly ticked on, and on, and on; asking themselves, are they alive, are they dead, who will get the winning hands and who will have to pay; not with money but with the most precious gift we possess? The lives of these trapped miners were in the balance, perhaps they were dead already. Only time will tell, and with the vengeance of a tornado moving down the valley. If hell can be described as waiting to know if your loved ones are alive or dead, this was living through hell. Their loved ones trapped in the hell hole beneath their feet, they were living in hell on the surface, wishing it was them down there instead, so that their loved ones would be safe.

Presently, the first piece of news was released: there were not fifteen, but twenty men unaccounted for, but it was believed that they were all trapped behind the fall. The rescue services were in the process of making the area safe for the rescue to commence. This news perked up PJ, and he stood up, regained his composure and offered his help to the rescue services. They needed volunteers, but declined PJ; he was too near the problem and would be better on the surface.

His wife, Joan, and their daughter, Samantha, arrived, and it was obvious they had been crying.

"They are all trapped and alive," PJ said, and kissed his wife and daughter. They placed their arms around each other for mutual comfort.

"Thank God, Phil, thank God," his wife kept repeating.

"Den will be alright. I just know it, daddy," his daughter said, but in a tone that suggested that she only half believed this.

Three people, riddled with fear, waited, contemplating the future but helpless to control the clouds of doom hanging over them, intoxicated with foreboding, fearing to receive news of their son and brother lying dead, deep in the ground. Such a plight would surely move even the trees to weep.

Chapter 28

FURTHER INFORMATION began to filter through; the area underground had been made secure, and volunteers were needed, to help to dig the men out. Every miner was ready; they would work until they dropped. Mog left PJ and went to get changed. People were still arriving, as the news spread. The police were already on the colliery, as well as a large number of colliery officials, and they were all needed, to control the ever increasing crowd.

Time moves at a constant speed, each second an exact replica of the one before and the one after, seamless and steady, never stopping, always moving forward. Time, for these people, waiting for news, seemed to have slowed and started to run backwards. Their thoughts were on yesterday, when they felt safe, away from this nightmare and living hell. Oh, how they wished for yesterday!

More news came after dusk. All the pit lights were turned on full. Other, larger lights were erected, and the whole area was floodlit. The rescue services had heard tapping along the rail that ran the length of the tunnel. This could only mean that the men were alive. This news brought a loud cheer from the crowd and a few of the women shouted, "Thank God, there is hope."

Many tons of rubble blocked the tunnel, and the amount of effort needed to move all this earth would be prodigious. It was expected that it might take a few days to dig out the tunnel. The main problems were now apparent: the danger of another roof fall, or explosion. The work would be slow. Concern was growing about how long the men could hold out without food and water, and about the amount of air left in the tunnel.

The night was now well advanced, and there was constant movement on the pit surface, with people arriving and departing. The whole pit top was covered with ambulances, police cars, fire engines and caravans, all on standby until needed. Tea and coffee were freely available as the canteen staff walked around, offering refreshments to anyone that asked. The mining community was again united in uncertainty, as the names of the missing men were disclosed. We already knew who they were but it was now official.

A number of working groups of twelve men worked for four hours at a time at the tunnel.

"I'll work till I drop," one of the men shouted.

There was no shortage of men, there were more on standby, waiting to volunteer, than there were in the working groups.

The night passed, and the following morning, George Thomas, our MP, turned up to see how the work was progressing and to lend his support to the families who were still awaiting developments. He spent most of the morning at the colliery, talking to everyone he met, and, then, he held a meeting with the pit manager, to discuss the progress being made, before moving back to London that evening.

More news arrived in the afternoon. The tapping from the trapped men was strong but it would be another day, if not two, before they expected the rescuers to reach the end of the tunnel and the men. The work was slow. Every few feet, they needed to stop, to secure the roof, before moving forward, and this was taking time and could not be rushed. Safety, in these conditions, must always come first. To further frustrate the situation, only three men could work at one time in the front of the tunnel, due to the limited amount of space. The men in this group changed every fifteen minutes, in a constant effort to move the work forward as quickly as possible.

Mog was in one of these groups, and my father was on standby, waiting to see if he would be needed. After his shift,

Mog called over at our house, offered a cigarette to my mother and said, "Things are not good down there. The whole of the tunnel has fallen down. If we do not reach the men shortly, there may not be enough air left for them to survive."

He offered a light to my mother and then lit his own cigarette. My father was sitting in the corner.

"It looks bad. Why did no one test for gas? There should be a test every hour, not once a week," he declared. Mog looked at him and agreed. He asked, "How is PJ? His boy is one of the trapped men; it's his only son, too."

"He's in a bit of a state. He has not left the colliery top since the accident happened, nor has his wife; his daughter has also stayed, only going away to fetch them food." Mog replied.

"This is a sad business. When the roof comes down, there is no where to run. Let's hope they all come out alive," my father said, as Mog went home, to snatch a few hours sleep before the next shift.

This was now the second night since the accident and there had been no further news, except for the constant tapping, which spurred the work forward as quickly as was possible without endangering anyone. The rescuers estimated that there was enough air trapped in the tunnel to last the men another day, two at the most, so things were now desperate. They needed a breakthrough and they needed it quickly, if the men were to be brought out alive.

The tunnel opening was enlarged and the work group size increased from twelve to fifteen, allowing five instead of three to work at the entrance, operating for half hour spells. We were all aware that time was running out, and nerves had begun to fray. Short, sharp answers were given to questions, and everyone wanted to be left alone. The worry was deep inside us all; we felt helpless, hopeless, and hypersensitive to everything and anything.

A body had been found in the tunnel, the first casualty,

crushed and mutilated, the face unrecognisable, a sacrifice to the power and strength of Black Gold. This hit us hard. The first hammer blow had been struck. We were now expecting more. We had thought and hoped that all the men were trapped, and were starting to believe that they would be all brought out alive. How many others would be found in the tunnel? There were still nineteen unaccounted for. Knocking could still be heard, but that could be from only one man. The despondency swept through our minds like a fog, killing expectation and hope. We now knew there was death in the hole, for certain, and the prospect of them all being alive had gone forever.

The dead man was named as John Williams from Pentre, a miner in his early forties, with three grown up boys and a daughter. The sudden shock showed in their faces as they were called to the ambulance room to be told the news that their father was dead, crushed when the roof fell in on top of him. A man in the wrong place at the wrong time, he had paid the ultimate price, his only mistake was trying to feed his family in the only way he knew how, by work, and now he was dead for his foolishness.

The watchers saw the body being carried over the pit. As the stretcher passed, there was silence and a feeling of deep despair. The women covered their faces, the tears ran down over their hands, the men removed their caps, heads bowed, as they stood upright, as a mark of respect for their dead colleague, pain clearly visible in their faces as their heartfelt sympathy went out to the dead man's family.

PJ and his wife stood silent, praying as the stretcher went past that their uncertainty would end shortly, and they would be with their son, alive; glad this stretcher was not his, yet still feeling for this family at this loss of their loved one. A few people congregated around PJ and his wife, and one of them said, "Your son will be alright. They say the knocking can be heard in several places. John Williams was right in the front of the tunnel; the rest of the men worked further back and are still behind the fall. The rescue teams are three quarters way through the tunnel and are planning to break through tomorrow morning."

Joan was the first to speak.

"Dennis, oh, my Dennis, I pray to God you are right, there is still hope."

PJ just stood and looked, tried to speak, but no words came; his daughter asked. "You say they are nearly through the tunnel and the rest are behind safe?"

"This is what I have heard. Tomorrow morning is the time, if there were more people in the tunnel, they would have found them by now," the same person replied.

"Why don't you go home, PJ, and take your wife with you; nothing is going to happen until tomorrow," another person suggested.

"Come on, Dad, let's go and get some sleep," his daughter said.

"I'm staying until I know one way or the other. Take your mother home. I'll be alright with the rest of the men. Joan, you go home. Get a few hours rest, and come back tomorrow," he said, looking sadly at his daughter and wife.

"Come on, mum, dad is right, let's get a few hours sleep." The girl led her mother to a waiting police car.

The pit was not as busy as earlier, the breakthrough would not happen until the next day, and a lot of the crowd went home for the night. The work teams were now within a short distance of where the men were trapped and could clearly hear them tapping and shouting. The breakthrough could not be made until the whole of the roof and surrounding area had been reinforced, in case there was another fall, and the rescue teams were taking no chances. Oxygen was being pumped into the tunnel, the immediate threat of suffocation was over, and it was prudent to secure the area before moving forward to complete the operation.

That night, the whole of Cwmparc was in sombre mood, everyone was concerned, yet hopeful that the men would all be rescued successfully. Tremains was the scene of apprehension and discussion, the men all talking about the hoped-for breakthrough the next day. The drinkers knew all the trapped men; some of whom were cousins, uncles or good friends. Hopes were high; no further casualties had been found in the tunnel and none were now expected. To further reinforce this feeling of optimism, the men spoke more loudly, but there was no celebration, they had been here before and did not wish to tempt fate before their work colleagues were totally safe above ground.

Mog entered the bar, followed by my father a few minutes later, and the death of John Williams was the main topic of conversation.

"Mog, you were underground at the time. Was he already dead on discovery?" one of the men asked, as he was about to order a pint of beer.

"Dead and cold. He was killed instantly, his head crushed flat. We only recognized him by the number on his lamp. It was found nearby," Mog answered.

"How was the rest of the body?" another enquired.

"How the bloody hell do you think the body looked? Burnt, totally crushed, unrecognisable, squashed he was, under the full fall of the roof. There was no chance of him surviving." Mog replied, with anger in his voice. "Even without the fall, he would have been killed. He took the full blast of the explosion before the roof came down on top of him. His body was extensively burnt in the explosion; death would have been instantaneous," Mog explained.

"This is a bad business. When something happens underground, there is no where to run or hide. We are all like trapped animals tethered by the feet, with the roof the bullet, handle ever ready on the trigger, waiting, ever waiting to give us its gift for disturbing its rest," my father said, as if talking to himself.

A few of the men nodded their heads in agreement.

"True, right, the roof is a bloody bullet always pointing at us, constantly waiting to discharge the power of death over us," another person in the gathering replied, carrying the bullet analogy further.

The landlord's wife walked over from the other end of the bar and asked, "Shall we organize a collection for the dead man?"

"No, not yet," Mog answered. "Let us get the rest out first, in case something else goes wrong."

Ron now joined the assembled crowd and commented, "The rest are at the end of the tunnel; if others were dead, we would have heard by now."

"May be so, may be so, but Mog is right, let's wait until all the men are on the surface and safe," my father said, as he sipped the last drop of beer and handed the glass to the landlady for a refill.

"What time tomorrow are they hoping to break through and complete the rescue? I hear they are only a few feet away and are talking with the trapped men."

"Early, everything is ready. They do not want me at the pit tomorrow. The last team will be going under about now, to complete the rescue," Mog announced, looking at his watch at the same time.

"Pity about old John Williams. If only he had not been in the tunnel when the explosion happened," someone said.

"Poor bugger, it was not his fault; he would have been dead before he knew there was anything wrong," another remarked.

"Come on, boys, it is time to go home. Drink your pints and I'll see you all tomorrow. Let's hope this sorry business will be over by then and we'll be able to have a bit of a celebration," the landlord said, while collecting the empty glasses off the bar.

The valley was quiet that night, everyone preoccupied with

the following day. It looked as if there would be only one casualty, but, as yet, no one was definite about this. Many prayers were said in many houses that night for the men trapped deep in the earth below, that they would be brought to the surface safe and alive.

Chapter 29

THE TRAPPED MEN WERE REUNITED with their rescuers at seven that morning. There had been a number of injuries, the most serious being fire blast from the explosion, and a number of burns, but none were life threatening. Two men had dislocated arms, a few had dislocated shoulders, one a crushed hand, and there were a few broken toes. The rest consisted mainly of minor cuts and bruises. The euphoria felt by the rescuers and the rescued was indescribable, all were congratulating themselves on a job well done. All nineteen men were accounted for, dirty, hungry, and in need of a bit of loving care and attention, but alive.

The freed men were immediately given water and attended to by the doctors and first aid team, who had been waiting underground to attend to the injured before the men were moved. The danger was not just from the visible injuries, but also from the shock and trauma they would have suffered after the explosion. This could be the main enemy in these situations, and so the medics were taking no chances. A lot of the men were tired and exhausted through lack of food and water, but it was better to be cautious and not take any chances. Methodical caution was the order of the day, even if the first indications were that injuries were slight.

A sense of relief swept through the valley as the news was relayed to the surface. The women were hugging and kissing each other and everyone else they could find. The men just stood and smiled, shaking each other's hands, and tapping each other on the backs, happy to know that their colleagues were now officially declared safe.

Happiness was all around, the valley was happy and merry, and there would be celebrations tonight. The women started to cry only when the likelihood of further casualties started to subside.

PJ's wife and daughter returned to the pit at six in the morning, both were overjoyed, their happiness was overflowing. Joan fell into her husband's arms, both of them crying with happiness that their Dennis was safe. The relief was immense, the cloud that hung heavy over them, numbing and blocking their passion for life, was at last drifting away to reveal the warmth and light of the sun that had been denied them these last few days.

"Thank you, God, oh, thank you for not taking my Dennis," PJ cried, looking up to the heavens and shouting, "My Dennis, my Dennis is alive, thank you, thank you, oh, God, my son is safe."

They were happy in the knowledge that, in a few hours, they would be reunited with their Dennis. PJ was shaking hands and inviting everyone to his house, for a party to celebrate his good fortune.

Mog and my father were also on the pit surface, talking about the explosion.

"It could have been avoided, with greater safety controls. I thought they were all goners and expected the worst, when the explosion happened," my father confessed.

"They are all lucky to escape alive. Things would have been different if the men had been in the tunnel," Mog replied.

"Tell that to the wife and children of John Williams. They see no luck in this situation," my father further remarked.

"Too true. He was crushed; the boys that found him say he was squashed flat, totally flat, one large stone inflicting all the damage," Mog replied.

"Yes, but he was killed by the explosion, not the roof fall," my father said. "They say his clothes were burnt so badly that they were welded to his bones, and the skin melted over them, to form one black mass. He looked like a large lump of coal," Mog said grimly.

"Don't be disrespectful, Mog," my father complained.

"I was just telling it as it was. His body was one black lump," Mog said, they walked past PJ.

PJ came straight over, shook them both by the hand, and invited them to a celebration party.

"Don't forget, PJ, that one man was killed. I will go to no celebration," my father scolded. "You were lucky, PJ. Show some respect for the family of the dead man," he added.

"Sorry, Dai, I just did not think. You are right. How could I have been so thoughtless? I got carried away with my own enthusiasm. I was just so happy that it was not my Dennis, and I gave no thought to anyone else. Forgive me, boys." He bowed his head in shame.

"That is totally understandable, PJ. You have nothing to reproach yourself over. I would feel the same way if it was my son. I, too, would wish to celebrate and would celebrate with you if John were still alive," my father said gently.

The families of the rescued men were all assembled on the pit surface, chatting and smiling happily while waiting for the men to surface and be reunited with their loved ones, the uncertainty over. They were coming home alive. It would be another three hours before they came up from the pit bottom.

"They're coming, they're coming," a woman shouted.

"No, they are members of the rescue team," another shouted.

"They are following behind. The first will be up in about twenty minutes," one in this group shouted, as they all made their way to the baths, to wash the dirt from their bodies. The expectation of the imminent arrival of the survivors lent an almost carnival atmosphere. Some people were shouting, other just stood and talked, a few of the children were dancing, picking up on the excitement of the moment.

The only family not on the pit top was the Williams. They

went home the night before, broken and grief stricken, alone with their thoughts, the head of their family no longer on this earth. Burned and crushed just for looking after the most important people in his life, his only crime was to work to give them a roof over their heads and to put food in their stomachs, his repayment was a cruel death. This family would not celebrate, only cry, and cry, for the loss of a husband and a father.

"Look, look, they are here. See. Look, everyone, see," the children shouted, having been the first to notice the stretchers coming from the pit cage. The injured were the first to be brought to the surface, four men with a stretcher carried Bill Davies, who had a broken shoulder.

"It's Bill, Bill Davies," a few men shouted.

His family rushed forward and tried to get to the stretcher simultaneously, holding his hand and hugging him; his wife kissed him on the cheek.

"Bill, I swear if you do this again, I'll bloody kill you, you old sod," she exclaimed, unaware of the irony of her words.

The rest of the men soon appeared, black, dirty, but all very much alive. As the stretchers were carried past the assembled crowd, the rush forward, the reuniting, the jubilation, the sheer happiness of the moment cannot be described in words.

Each woman caressed her man; children hugged their fathers, not caring how filthy they looked as the dirt rubbed off into them. Dirt can be washed away. The stretchers moved into the daylight, the rest of the men walking behind. They were coming out of the hellhole into the light, the light a lot of them thought they would never see again. The brightness blinded them after the darkness they had been in for so long.

"Come on boys, it's good to see you all again. Well done, well done," people shouted as the rest of the group filed past.

A few minutes later, two men ran excitedly out of the ambulance room, one of them shouting loudly, "John Williams.

I've just seen him. He is alive; alive I say. He is in the baths, as large as life."

"No. I do not believe it, he could not have survived under that fall," another cried in disbelief.

"He is in the shower room. I've not only seen him, but also spoken to him, and he is no ghost; he is walking, talking and happy to be out of the pit," the speaker confirmed.

The other man said, "John was not in the tunnel, but right at the back, and there is not even a scratch on him."

"This is good news. The family are at home, all in a state of shock. There will be a party in the Williams' house tonight."

A few cheers were heard coming from the crowd, who had heard of John's good fortune.

"He has more lives than a cat," someone of the crowd remarked.

Another shouted, "Three cheers for John."

The crowd was overwhelmed, lost in the excitement as the news quickly spread over the pit surface. John, as far as they were concerned, had been returned to them from the dead.

"If it was not John, who was in the tunnel?" another asked, looking shocked.

"They are just checking on the situation and will let us know as soon as possible. A police van has already been sent to the Williams' house, to inform them of the good news," said an official, crossing over into the ambulance room.

In this lottery of life, what is good news for the Williams family is a tragedy for another family. The charred and flattened body was still to be identified. The worms will feast, if not on John, on some other person. What family will be called into the ambulance room? We all suspected that we knew, but would not say, and then the call went out.

"Would Philip John please come to the ambulance room immediately."

The shock suddenly hit the assembled crowd, and they all fell silent, the excitement stilled as they looked for PJ.

To watch this family moving across the pit surface, slowly, so slowly, forward towards the ambulance room and into tomorrow, was heart-rending. There were no shouts or cheers now; the jubilation was gone as these three people waited to be told what they already knew, but by walking slowly, tried to keep Dennis alive in their minds a while longer. They were walking as if they were going to be hanged, each step measured precisely. We all saw them enter the ambulance room and pass out of our sight.

It does not take long to tell a family that a son is dead; on this occasion, it took less than four minutes. When they emerged back into the open air, tears were running freely down PJ's face. He held the hands of his wife and daughter. The three walked towards a waiting police car, supporting one another in deep felt grief. Their heartfelt agony cried into the air, as deep feelings of pain surfaced, tearing at the fibre of this family and threatening its very existence. This silent mocking seemed to be playing a tune around them, the stillness of the moment acted as a shroud. The melody silently played on this piano in the sky was for Dennis. The song was a tribute to the power of Black Gold. Three people, forlorn in their own thoughts, entered the car, to be taken home to memories of a loved one who was gone forever.

The crowds were starting to disperse, thinking of how PJ and his family must be feeling. Mog lit a cigarette, turned to my father, and said, "This will be hard for him. Father and son were close and were always together on a Saturday night, in the Stag Hotel."

My father turned to Mog and replied, "This would be hard on any one, Mog, a son gone before the father. This is not the way. We should not have to bury our own children. The unfairness of the way we have to live is not right, you know; there must be a better way."

They walked off the pit and in through back door that my mother had already opened.

The funeral was held a few days later, and most of the pit employees turned out to say their farewells to young Dennis. Joan outlived her son by six weeks, and died of a heart attack, or so the death certificate stated, but the general consensus was that she died of a broken heart. PJ never recovered from the loss of a son and a wife, all in a matter of a few weeks. He went to live with his daughter, a broken man. Often, he could be heard lamenting how he was robbed of his Joan before her time, and complaining that it should have been him who was taken, not Dennis.

Chapter 30

THE FOLLOWING WEEK, the pit returned to normal and it was work as usual. It was not long before I was back into mischief and looking for new adventure and excitement. The den had been discovered by Mr Parry and destroyed. Each time we tried to build a new den, it would be discovered and destroyed, continually frustrating us in our plans. The pit surface was getting too hot for us and we needed to rethink our strategy and come up with an alternative site for a den.

A few days later, an opportunity presented itself, whereby we could have a den away from the pit surface, and in relative security from being caught by adults. A few doors down from our house, an old lady had recently died, leaving the house empty. She had only one son and he lived away, so the house was up for sale.

At the bottom of the garden was a shed that was attached to the outdoor toilet and extended along the bottom wall by the back door. I thought this could be our new den. The trouble was, the back door was locked, and I could not open it from the back lane. The only alternative would be to scale the wall, get into the back yard, and open the back door from the inside.

The problem with this plan was the fact that the other houses overlooked the garden. If I scaled the back wall, the risk would be high that the neighbours would not only stop me, but also tell my parents, and so caution would be needed to bring my plan to fruition.

I needed to get into the back garden, and the only way to do this was to throw a ball over the wall, and then to go around to the front of the house, knock at the next-door neighbour's house, and ask for my ball back. I was let into the house and told to go and look for the ball in the back garden.

"The ball is next door," I shouted back.

"Jump over the wall and get the ball."

Being an obedient sort of person, I immediately complied and scrambled into the garden, safe in the knowledge that it was done with adult approval. The garden was overgrown with weeds and a few small bushes, and I pretended to look around for the ball, thrashing at the weeds and grass as I went along.

The ball was on the pathway, and I kicked it down the garden and into the shed. In the shed, I unlocked the back door, tied up the handle, so it would not fall back into place, climbed back into the other garden, thanked the neighbour and walked out through the front of his house, with my ball safely tucked under my arm. The first part of the plan was now complete.

The following evening, I entered by the back door and started to construct the den in the shed and toilet. There were a few tons of coal in the shed but there was still room for several people to sit next to the toilet in relative safety, without being seen from any of the other houses overlooking the garden. The problem was that I could not use any candles or torches in the shed, only in the toilet area, in case the neighbours saw the light.

I did not for one minute think about trespassing and the consequences of entering a property illegally. The old lady was dead, so where is the harm? The only thing that mattered to me was to construct a den. This was of the utmost importance.

I would jam the back door closed by wedging a piece of wood under the door and closing it tightly. To anyone passing, the door would look locked and, providing I was careful and there was no one around in the lane when I entered and departed, everything would be all right.

I wanted the whole thing in place before the gang was informed, and I made a few trips back and forth, in order to get everything ready. I obtained candles and placed them carefully in the toilet, lighting them after closing the toilet door, to make sure no light could be seen from the outside. I was now prepared to inform the gang. Excitedly, I ran out of the back door and straight into Mr Parry.

"Why are you in the back of this house?" he asked in a stern voice.

"Getting my ball," I replied.

"I see no ball!"

"I, I could not find it. The whole garden is overgrown and it was only a small ball."

"How did you get into the garden?"

"The door was open and I just walked in. Someone must have left it open. It's lucky I found the door open. I was just going around the front to see the neighbours next door and tell them. Would you like to come with me?" I asked, thinking fast.

"Is there any mess in the back, or any signs that the house has been broken into?" he asked.

"No, definitely not. There are a few candles that I noticed just now, when I used the toilet," I remarked, trying to cover my back before the candles were discovered. "It is lucky I lost my ball, or no one would have known the back door was open, and the house could have been robbed. Shall I go and lock the door from the inside and jump over the wall?" I enquired innocently.

"Good idea."

A minute later, the door was locked, and I was back over the wall, next to Mr, Parry, as we walked up the lane.

This definitely had been a close shave. I could feel the razor moving across my skin. Of all the people to bump into, he was the one I most wished to avoid. My plan was now in ruins. There was no way the toilet and garden shed could be used as a den. It was far too dangerous. I needed a new plan and was fast running out of ideas.

It was decided to concentrate now on getting a part time job or, at any event, to work for money. That evening, when we were all together, Deadeye had a brain wave. To be fair to him, he had been eating a lot of cabbage recently, and I put the idea down to this.

"We should go round the pigeon loft owners, ask if they are having trouble with rats and offer to use our ferrets to flush them out into the open," he explained. "Our dogs could catch and kill the rats, and we could charge the pigeon owners for every rat we caught," he elaborated.

Kevin must have also been nibbling, not on cabbage, but on large quantities of sawdust, because he also had a brain wave. "Why don't we breed a few rats and let them loose near the pigeon lofts, and charge the pigeon owners, when we catch them," he proposed, excited about his idea.

Deadeye shook his head. "They have enough rats of their own; they wish to rid themselves of the rats, they do not require us to give them more."

"I was only being businesslike and trying to make us more money," Kevin retorted.

"More money, more money!" Gerald shouted, pulling at his hair as if shocked by Kevin's brain wave. "If the allotment owners and the pigeon owners heard we were planning this, it would not be more money they would give us but they'd bury us five feet under, and feed us to the rats."

David then chipped in as Kevin was about to develop his brain wave further. "Kevin, be quiet. Don't mention this again, in case you are overheard and it gets out that we are rat breeders instead of rat catchers. No, Kevin, shut up," he shouted. Kevin just looked at the four of us, sat down on the floor and said no more on the subject.

One thing we were all agreed upon was the money we could all earn. Rat catching could be a good source of income for us but we could not decide how we would distribute the money we earned. Eventually, it was resolved to share all revenue equally, after the cost of the cartridges we used from the small-bore shotgun was deducted. This gun Deadeye had recently acquired, and it was far more effective and a lot more deadly than the pellet gun he had used up until then.

Rats were a constant menace to pigeon fanciers, a nuisance they could do without. The rats raided the pigeon nests, took the eggs and killed the young pigeon chicks. Pigeon fanciers were always on their guard against rats. This battle would be continuous; they would always be looking for ways to exterminate the vermin, and, from our point of view, prepared to pay for the service.

There were five of us in the team and we would be called The **Rat Destroy Team**. Not all of us had our own ferrets; David and Kevin were destroyers without portfolio, because the rest of us had at least one ferret each. We were classified as destroyers with portfolio. Deadeye objected to this, and wanted a distinct classification for himself because he had the largest ferret, a small bore shotgun, and a dog. Finally, it was agreed he would be referred to as **vermin destroyer with portfolio extraordinary**, leaving Gerald and me with the same title minus the word extraordinary.

The two dogs in the team were Russ and Bull's-eye. They would catch the rats after the ferrets flushed them out into the open. The dogs caught the rats in their mouths and killing them with one bite, before moving on to the next rat.

Brian and I were always disagreeing about which dog was the most effective. He even wanted his dog to be known as Bull's-eye Extraordinary. I eventually agreed to this, so long as my dog could be referred to as Russ, The Rat Destroyer. A scorecard would be used, to keep a tally, and marked up after every new rat caught. The average number caught in an afternoon was a dozen and the most we ever caught at one time was over twenty.

We were definitely making a name as exterminators, and were often approached by allotment owners and asked to spend a day in their gardens, plying our skills for our usual charge. We never seemed to make a lot of money, because what we earned would be spent on sweets or snacks, often before we arrived home.

On one particular ratting expedition, we were called to a pigeon loft behind Vicarage Terrace. The owner was having difficulty with large brown rats, and was losing a number of young chicks. Poison could not be used because the birds could eat it, so the only alternative was to call us in to solve the problem.

We arrived early on a Sunday morning, and intended to use the ferrets around the garden perimeter first, thereby forcing the rats we did not catch at the first attempt to come into the centre of the garden, to be caught later. The two dogs were held near to where we felt the rats would emerge from their holes, one dog held by Deadeye, the other ready by me, ready to let go as soon as the rats were out in the open.

The ferrets would be placed into the rat burrows at the outer end, to drive the rats into the garden, to be caught immediately by the dogs. If they escaped this first round, they would be trapped under the pigeon shed, or under old sheets of corrugated iron, left at the corner near the centre of the allotment. We knew exactly where the rats would be hiding, and would sort them out later.

The first round was a total success. David and Gerald placed the ferrets down into the burrows, and Kevin was left on standby, to see where the larger concentration of rats ran to, when they bolted.

Within a minute, the action started, with rats running everywhere; wave after wave tumbled out of the holes and ran in all directions. Our trusted dogs moved from one to the other, biting at them and tossing them aside in order to tackle the next one. This first round we bagged at least a dozen, and at least double this number got away. We were all very pleased with ourselves. We would hit a new record today, and felt excited about the prospect. There were more rats concentrated in this small area than we had ever seen before. No wonder the owner was having problems.

We caught several more as the day progressed, and we decided to take a rest and eat our packed lunches before the afternoon sport started. We wanted to tackle the area around the corrugated iron and the pigeon loft next. We knew there were large concentrations of rats in this area, besides the ones that the dogs were unable to catch in the first wave.

Over lunch, we devised a plan to flush out the vermin in different sections, and because of the numbers involved, we decided to use the small bore shot gun to shoot some as they came out of their hiding holes. We only had two dogs, and they would be working flat out. By shooting a few as well, we would be able to bag more altogether.

The only person available to hold the gun was Kevin. The rest of us were looking after the dogs, or ferrets, and were unable to concentrate on holding the gun and shooting when the rats bolted. Reluctantly, and against his better judgment, Deadeye handed over his trusted gun to Kevin, with strict instructions on how to use it and a dire warning always to point it at the ground for safety, and to shoot only when he saw a rat, providing we and the dogs were nowhere near.

He allowed Kevin a few shots at the floor and nearby tins, to feel how the trigger action works and to sample the recoil after the gun is fired. I could see he was very uneasy about having Kevin in charge of his gun, but it was Kevin or no one, so he went along reluctantly with the situation. Deadeye was not relaxed; he was showing all the signs of uneasiness. "This is not a toy, Kevin. Be careful, and watch for us and the dogs. Don't point at them, even when the gun is empty. If you are not sure, Kev, let the rat get away."

"Don't worry, I know what to do. Stop keeping on all the

time. Do you think me a fool?" Kevin asked, rather agitated at not being trusted.

In the ferrets went, out the rats came, one after the other. We let the dogs loose into the centre of them, and with teeth snapping in all directions, they began to toss them one-way and then the other. The ground was alive with rats, some brown, others black, some small, a few large, moving like ants across the floor, running for their lives, as the dogs followed in a frenzy of killing.

The excitement of the situation was electric. We tried to hit the rats with our feet and with sticks we picked up for the purpose, shouting at each other and at the dogs all in the same instant. The commotion was all around us. One of the rats even jumped up on Gerald's back, trying to get away in the commotion, and fell back to the ground, only to be caught in the mouth of Bull's-eye, while Deadeye looked on in admiration.

A shot from the gun rang out, followed by a loud shout. I looked round and saw Kevin drop the gun to the floor and look down at what he had just shot. Bull's-eye lay on the floor, shot through the back of the neck. The dog's four legs were all moving back and forth from the sudden shock. He was still alive, but only just, and bleeding heavily from the wound. Deadeye was around the other side of the shed, and did not at first realise his dog had been shot, until I shouted, "Kev, what have you done? Brian, Brian, come quick, it's Bull's-eye; your dog is bleeding."

Gerald ran forward and David leaned over the dog, as if to try and stem the bleeding. The whole of the neck and head were covered in blood. Deadeye ran towards his trusted animal, leant down by the side of his dog, and placed his hands around its neck, as if trying to stop the bleeding.

"What has happened? Oh, Bull's-eye, what have they done? You will be alright." He cried out in obvious agony, looking at the dog, his hands now covered in blood from the wound. The sudden reality had now set in and tears were starting to roll off his cheeks while he held his trusted friend Bull's-eye close to his face.

Gerald tried to take the dog from Brian, but he would not let the animal go. I placed my arm around his shoulder, to try to give him some comfort, but he did not move. He stood rigid, holding the dog ever tighter to his chest, as if he possessed the power to make the wound go away. It was obvious that the dog could not survive. It was breathing heavily and the blood flowing from the neck could not be stopped.

"You idiot, you stupid fool, Kev. How could you pull the trigger when the dog was next to the gun! Look what you have done," I shrieked at him on the top of my voice.

Kevin, in shock, stared at the gun and swayed back and forth in a rocking movement. "I did not see the dog. I did not see Bull's-eye. I'm sorry. The corgi came from nowhere. I did not see. I honestly did not see. Sorry, Brian, sorry, Brian, please, I'm sorry." He kept on repeating this, until we shouted at him to shut his stupid mouth, which he promptly did and walked away.

The dog was now dead, and we all tried to console Brian. I moved forward and took the dog from him. The others held him by the shoulders and tried to get him to sit down on the grass. I wrapped the dog in my jacket and placed him on the ground, completely covered. Brian was inconsolable and was starting to get angry, especially with Kevin. David walked over to Kevin and told him to make himself scarce. He told Kevin to take the gun with him, and stay far away from Brian.

We retrieved the ferrets, and Russ, my dog, just looked on, wondering what had happened.

"I loved that dog. He was mine. I reared him from a pup and now he is dead," Brian yelled, the tears falling down his face. "Where is Kev?"

"He has gone, Brian," David answered.

"It is all his fault. I warned him about the danger, and I did not want to give him my gun. I knew something would happen. I just knew it. How could he mistake my dog for a rat? A tooth for a tooth, I say. He shot my dog, and now I will shoot him. Where is he? I'll shoot him in the neck, see how he likes it."

"What good will that do?" Gerald asked.

"He won't be able to shoot another dog," Brian said, and no one could disagree with that, but to shoot Kevin, with that objective in mind, was definitely rather extreme.

"Don't shoot him yet. Sort out everything first, take the dog home and rest up for a while. There will be plenty of time to shoot Kev later." David said, trying to defuse the situation and give Brian time to think what he intended to do. David hoped that time would change his mind.

"You are in shock. Let's go home," I told him.

"Where is the gun? I need my gun," Brian insisted.

"The gun is in a safe place. I will drop it off at your house later," Gerald promised.

"Come on, Brian, let's go home." I pulled him onto his feet. David picked up the dog, and the four of us walked to Brian's house, carrying the dead dog in turns. Brian was still determined to exact his revenge on the hapless Kevin. After we left Brian's house, two of us went to find Kevin and warned him to lie low for a few days. We took the gun from him, intending to hide it from Brian for a while.

"He is going to shoot you, Kev, if he catches you, so make sure you are not around until he cools down. He is upset and angry at the moment, and blames you for the death of his dog, so keep out of his way."

Brian was more than capable of causing serious damage to Kevin, in his state of mind. He loved Bull's-eye, his corgi, and was incapable of being reasoned with. He was after revenge, and no amount of reasoning would change his mind. His behaviour was totally irrational, and he could be capable of anything for a while.

The following day, he was still in deep shock. His face looked numb as he watched his father bury the dog in the garden. I called down to his house, to see how he was, and met his father on the doorstep. I told him that I would bring the gun back later.

"He is in the garden and very upset about the death of his dog," his father told me, and asked for my version of events and how the dog was shot. "Guns are too dangerous when you are out with the ferrets and dogs. Bring the gun to me and I will lock it away."

This was just the news I needed, and I immediately retrieved the gun from my house and handed it to Brian's father. After this, I went down the garden to look for Brian. I could see where the dog was buried. Brian was in a better state of mind than I anticipated, but still very much upset about the death of his trusted corgi.

"I've given the gun to your father. He is going to lock it away."

"Yes, he said that he wants to take the gun and lock it away until I am older," Brian said.

"Does that mean you are not going to shoot Kev," I asked hopefully, thinking the matter could now be laid to rest.

"Kev is a murderer, he killed my dog in cold blood, and he is not getting away with it," he growled, pulling out of the shed a large knife that he immediately started to sharpen. "I'm going to skin him alive and string him up for the birds."

"It's Kev's birthday shortly. Can't you wait until after the party? We are all invited, as you know. Kev has managed to get hold of a flagon of cider for us to drink, and it would be a pity if you skinned him first," I pleaded, knowing he enjoyed a cider shandy. "Why don't you talk to Kev?" I asked. "There may be another way to get your revenge, other than skinning him.

Perhaps something could be worked out."

"The only talk I intend to do is with this," Brian said, holding up the knife and waving it over his head.

"He is part of the gang. Wait until you talk to him," I pleaded, in one last attempt, but Brian's mind was made up and there was no way he would listen to reason.

Chapter 31

WHEN I CALLED at Vicarage Terrace, Kevin answered the door; I saw that he had shaved his hair.

"You are practically bald, Kev. Have you got nits?" I laughed. He looked ridiculous with short hair. He loved his old hairstyle, and for him to have shaved it off meant that something must be really wrong with his hair.

"I have done this as an act of respect, and as punishment for what I accidentally did to Brian and his dog," he stuttered, looking at me to see if there was any forgiveness in my eyes.

"Brian is only going to skin you alive. His gun has been taken off him, so you are safe against being shot," I blabbered. "I think he intends to skin you, but the way your hair looks, I think you have started without him." I added, laughing, trying desperately to keep a straight face.

"Here, take this to Brian as a peace offering." He handed me a paper bag with his hair inside. "Show this to him and tell him I am sorry," he continued, in a quiet voice. Kevin was really upset with the situation, and was doing all he could to show how he felt, trying desperately to get Brian to forgive him.

The following evening, after school, I went down to see Brian, to find out why he was not in school that day. I found him in the house, with a heavy cold. He was sitting in the corner of his front room with a blanket wrapped around him, looking really miserable and tired.

"I feel awful. I was up all night, coughing and sneezing, and I feel exhausted and worn out," he mumbled. "I can't see me getting to school this week. I can hardly walk, with this cold."

The truth of the matter was that, after the death of his dog, he was still in shock, and this was his way of handling the loss of Bull's-eye. I could see that he had been crying, his face was all puffy and blotched, but I said nothing about that, and asked him if I could get him anything for his cold.

"Could you feed my ferrets for a few days?" he asked.

I agreed to the request and left him in the chair, feeling dejected and sorry for himself.

The next few days were quiet and I did not go to see Kevin or Brian. I fed Brian's ferrets but I left it to him to contact me when he felt ready. On the Friday of that week, Brian called at my house. He was looking a lot better. He thanked me for looking after his ferrets and handed me a few toffees from his pocket, which I eagerly accepted, placing one into my mouth immediately.

"How is Kevin?" he asked, speaking with gentleness in his voice.

"Feeling terrible." It seemed the correct thing to say, although I really had no idea.

"Is he still having his party tomorrow?"

"I think so, but he is feeling really down about what happened. Apart from cutting his hair short, he does not know what else to do to make amends," I said. I was still hoping there could be reconciliation without a skinning taking place. "Kev will be with David, at his house, in a little while. They will be in the back yard. We could call to see them later, if you like," I suggested, hoping he would leave his knife at home. At that moment, David and Kevin walked around the corner by my house, and stopped when they saw Brian and me standing at my door.

"How are things, boys?" David asked.

Brian looked at Kevin, I could feel the tension between them and the uneasiness of the unexpected encounter. Kevin spoke first. "How are you feeling? I hear you have been down with a cold. Are you better now?"

"Oh, awe." There was silence for a few seconds. "All right now. It's your birthday tomorrow, if I'm not mistaken," Deadeye said uncertainly.

Kevin smiled. "You are invited and can sit next to me, if you like," he said, feeling a bit bolder at Brian's response.

The skinning threat was over and the friendship was renewed, to the relief of us all. Brian attended the party, the episode of the dog was put to rest once and for all, and we were friends again. The gang was reunited.

Chapter 32

SINCE THE INCIDENT with the insulation in the roof, my mother had kept quiet about any alterations to the house; she was still smarting from the mess she had experienced a few months earlier, and would not complain about anything to do with draughts or ceilings, in front of Mog. The one thing she kept mentioning was the inconvenience of going out to the bottom of the garden every time she needed to go to the toilet. Her theme was: how steep the steps were down into the garden; how they would be the death of her when the cold weather and snow came around again.

"We are not getting any younger, things will have to change," she remarked to anyone who would listen.

A few of the neighbours were having indoor toilets installed in their houses, and my mother was taken with the idea of visiting the toilet in the warmth of the house, instead of outside in the garden. She did not ask directly for an indoor toilet, but started to drop strong hints. "The Jones family have just brought their toilet indoors. What do you think, Dai?" she asked, after my father had just eaten his evening meal.

"These new ideas! It is not healthy to have a toilet inside the house. Keep all smells out in the open, where they belong."

"I knew you would agree. It is a good idea. Yes, we need to think about it. That is right, Dai, isn't it, but don't tell Mog." She had not been listening to what my father actually said, but heard what she wished to hear.

"Ay, ay, Reen, we will see," he replied, lit his pipe, sat back in the chair and closed his eyes, as if to say, I have turned off, my light is out, do what you like.

"She turned to me and said, "Your father is right; he is getting too old to go down the back garden every time he needs to go to the toilet. It's not right. What do you say?" Before I could say anything, she started again. "The cold weather will be with us again in a few months, and we must have an inside toilet for Dai before then. He insists.""

"But, mam, dad said he prefers the toilet left where it is, not indoors," I quickly replied, before she had time to start the next sentence.

"Don't be silly, you are too young to understand," she snapped. "Don't you think I know what he wants? He needs an indoor toilet, and an indoor one he is going to have. He is not aware of it, just yet," she added, confirming by this remark that she heard exactly what he had said.

My father winked at me, as if to say, what is the point in speaking, when your mother takes not the slightest notice? She interprets according to what she feels should be said, not what is actually said. It looked as if we were to have an indoor toilet; my father apparently demanded one, as she would later inform the neighbours.

It did not take Mog long to hear of the plan, and he came over to the house, to speak to my mother about the proposed innovation.

"What the hell do you need a toilet in the living room for?" he asked, rather shocked with the suggestion.

"Dai is not getting any younger, you know, and there are a few people bringing the toilet up from the back garden," she said sharply.

"The place for a toilet is in the back garden, not in the house. Cows shit where they stand and then lay in it; we go from the house to the end of the garden, into the open air. Civilized people do not foul their own nest. Have a bit of respect, for goodness sake, old girl," Mog argued, in an agitated voice.

"Don't call me old girl. Dai needs a toilet in the house and he will have one, so there," she shouted, stamping her feet.

"He never mentioned this to me before. He always seemed to like the toilet outside," Mog insisted, rather perplexed that my father would make such a request. "Even birds leave the nest to go to the toilet, but you want to stay where you are and smell the house out."

My mother was feeling trapped by this argument and needed to convince Mog of the rationale of the indoor toilet, or there would be pressure from all corners to abandon the project.

"You got it wrong, Mog. An indoor toilet means an extra toilet; the outdoor one is used for you know what, and the indoor one for the other."

"Other what?"

"You know: one toilet for one and the other for the ..., you know."

"Do you mean one to shit in and the other to wee in?" Mog asked loudly.

"Yes. Can you now see what Dai means? What do you think of his idea? It will do away with the piss pot under the bed," my mother continued, while her brother was processing this last remark.

"I can see where Dai is coming from. The number of times I have filled the piss pot in the middle of the night and had to take it downstairs and up the back, to empty it out and clean it before it can be used again; it is a regular occurrence after a night down the Legion," Mog agreed.

My mother was quick to further this advantage. She asked, "Why don't you have a toilet indoors, as well as Dai? You have plenty of room in the conservatory, next to the bath in the corner." My mother felt Mog weakening.

"The toilet would act as a sink, instead of me having to keep going up the back. There are no flies on Dai. A permanent indoor piss pot, it's a brilliant idea!" Mog exclaimed.

My mother had won the day, by attributing the brilliant idea to her husband. They say men have the upper hand. I never saw this when my mother wanted something. She would display the guile of the fox and the wisdom of the old owl, when it came to providing something that would be of benefit to her and the family.

In a matter of weeks, the toilet was installed in the overhang that, until now, had been used as a larder. A small conservatory was also built out to the end of the steps that lead down into the garden. This provided extra space for a sink unit, two small chairs and a cooker. There was also enough room in the larder to place a small bath; a door blocked off the whole area inside.

This made a big improvement to the way we lived, and my mother would proudly show off the new addition to anyone that entered the house. Even the milk and bread man were invited to use the toilet, when they called to deliver their produce, and whether they needed to use it was irrelevant, they were still marched in by my mother. The modern age had arrived in our house, and there would be no more frozen bottoms at the end of our garden. The outdoor toilet was quickly rendered obsolete.

Chapter 33

GIRLS INCREASINGLY TOOK UP more of our thoughts and conversation. Since the accident underground, the security at the pit was stepped up, and there was no way we were able to build a den. Even if we managed to do so without being spotted, the following day it would be found and destroyed, rendering the exercise futile. We were growing older; the main focus of attention was now on the opposite sex; we wanted what they had, but they wished to keep it to themselves. There was not a lot we could do about that, other than be nice to them and hope that they would relent in time.

The problem was, that they all had fathers, who knew exactly what we were after and did not like it one bit. If the girls flirted with us, their fathers were never far behind, keeping an eye on them and us, and discouraging any physical contact. We had given up any idea of trickery; whatever we tried, they would be a match for us and would outsmart us at every corner. In my mother I had a good role model on the wiles of the fairer sex and knew how clever they were, so we decided that the only way forward was to start courting.

We were unsure exactly what courting meant, but we knew a'courting we must go. Life was changing for us; we were in the process of transformation from child to adolescent and were confused about the physical changes we were experiencing. We were aliens to ourselves, and felt that our bodies were not our own, but belonged to someone else. Our hands were clammy and our bodies would be responsive, whenever we came within range of any smell linked with the girls. Our young, changing flesh seemed to be drawn to the girls like a bee to a flower. We were the bees and wished to drink deep to make honey with the girls. We knew where the flowers were, but we were still too young to know how to extract the nectar. It was needed, to quench the fire surging through our bodies at the speed of light.

While we did not know how to drink the nectar, our thirst for it was growing daily. We knew that the girls held the key and that it was up to us to open the door and make the honey flow.

We could not control these urges. It felt good to be alive, to breathe, to sing, and to dance into the air as if playing with the wind. We were at the threshold of something mysterious, magical, wonderful, and wanted more. Nature held us in its grip, compelling each of us to seek a partner. It was all new to us, although it had always been this way, when children become adults and experience what we were experiencing. It was the ritual that ensured the survival of our species, and we were enjoying every minute of it.

I liked Pat and thought the direct approach would be the best. I asked her outright if I could take her out courting. The answer was short and direct. "No, my father warned me against boys. They are after only one thing."

"What one thing is that?" I asked, looking all innocent.

"You know exactly what, so don't come the innocent with me," she told me sharply.

These girls are too bright for their own good, I thought. "I would like to spend some time with you. You know I like you." I answered.

"But, why do you like me?" she asked, looking straight at me as she spoke these words.

This is hard work I thought. "Because you are my friend and I like being with you," I replied.

"Why do you want to be my friend?"

By now, I felt like calling her the enemy, but I just smiled and kept calm. "I find you very beautiful and pleasant to be with." I was starting to feel embarrassed about the way the conversation was developing.

"I find you pleasant to be with and like your company also," she admitted quietly.

A breakthrough, I thought, as I could feel the juices stirring in my body. "Can ..., can we start courting?" I asked tentatively, nodding my head to help her with the reply.

"Maybe, but you will have to ask my father first," she said.

This was the last thing I wanted. How could she be so darned difficult? "Does that mean yes?" I persisted, ignoring the last remark and nodding my head again to help her make a positive response.

"It means, ask my father. I will invite you to tea and then you can ask him," she told me firmly.

Why must all girls have fathers? I had the feeling that I had been out smarted yet again. The following day, when I was in the garden, helping my father to trim the hedge, I asked him about girlfriends and what I needed to do to acquire one for myself.

"You can't acquire one like you would purchase a ferret or a dog," he replied.

"How do you catch one, then?"

"You can't catch one either; they catch you," he replied.

This made partial sense, because they always seemed to work everything to their own advantage. They had a way of keeping us in line without overtly doing anything. It's as if they knew they were the flowers and we needed the nectar, but, before they let us in, we had to buzz about amorously until they were ready.

"They throw out the fishing line and catch us on their hook," my father added.

"I'm pretty desperate to get on the hook," I told him.

"Just wait, be patient, and things will happen, just you wait and see," he advised, smiling to himself at my claim to desperation. "Come and help here," he said, pointing at the hedge, "and do some work. It will take your mind off growing up. Stay a child for as long as you can. You will be grown up for the rest of your life. Don't rush the process; there will be time enough for adult things in the future." He handed me the shears and lit his pipe.

The log den gone, the pit out of limits due to all the extra security, the house den locked and out of bounds since the incident with Mr. Parry, and no girl friend until I had been checked out by Pat's parents: things were taking a turn for the worse. The only thing left was to take the ferrets ratting, and, since the death of Bull's-eye, we had no inclination for this.

Chapter 34

APART WAY UP the Fishing River, about half way up on the left hand side of the mountain were a few dozen large, ancient oak trees, which we referred to as the old forest. These trees were all that remained in the valley that had once been covered by them. A large, mature oak always holds a mystery. These trees were standing here before the pits came, and if they could talk, what a tale they might tell, of how this valley looked before its beauty was destroyed by coalmining.

We regarded this patch of ancient forest as our play area. We knocked footholds into the living wood and used them to scale the trees. Ropes were thrown over the branches and used as swings. A stick acted as a seat, and we were ready to swing out as far as we were able, like the pendulum of a clock.

We were forever falling off the rope, bruising ourselves in the process, or being dragged across the ground, scraping our skin and ripping our clothes. This was fun. We had not a care in the world; our world was under the oaks. Silver and white light beams darted down through the leaves, bouncing and dancing off the branches and hitting the ground, flooding the dappled earth in bright colours.

Specks of dust could be seen twirling in the light beams, looking like microscopic wood fairies, guarding these wonderful trees by dancing in the air. There was beauty and mystery in every moment as we watched the sun's thin rays.

Climbing to the top of these large trees was dangerous and we often took foolhardy risks that, if they had gone wrong, could have resulted in serious injury, or even death. Danger was something that we all found acceptable and forgot about, until one of us fell and got hurt. We scaled the trees to the very canopy, knocking large nails into the wood as we climbed, to act as hand and foot grips. We tied ropes at different levels, to act as resting stations. We tied these ropes around us when we stopped to rest, knowing that we might have been in danger of falling off when we relaxed in the branches.

In some strange way, we felt safe at the top of these trees. There was calmness in being so close to these giants that we all felt comfortable about. The trees held us safe from the dangers of the pit and our own recklessness, and yet, they could turn their mighty wooden hands in an instant, and we would fall to the ground, like a leaf but a lot faster and with potentially fatal consequences.

Looking down over the valley from this lofty vantage point, the view it afforded was quite spectacular. We could see the pit, the sawmill, the river running past, the wagons waiting to be loaded, the endless patterns of rail track covering the pit surface, the pithead baths, the canteen, and the workmen, who looked like little ants, scurrying across the surface of the pit, going about their daily work. Standing above all these were the pit stack and the winder. Even from up here, they dominated the scene below, in all their ugliness.

One day, I felt a slight pain in my right side but did not pay much attention to it. I had experienced this niggling pain several times before, and it always went after a while. This time, I started to climb an old oak tree that I had climbed many times before. The footholds were familiar to me and I expected to reach the canopy without any trouble. The climb normally took about twenty minutes, allowing for a few rest stops on the way. I was about two thirds of the way up the tree when the pain started, slowly at first but getting stronger with every footstep. This pain was sharp and getting sharper, in the right side of my lower abdomen, sometimes moving around to the lower back, and now throbbing relentlessly. I could feel my body bending over, and found difficulty in holding on to the tree as the pain took a firmer hold. I could not go forward and I could not go back, my only option was to stay where I was. As the pain increased in severity, my vision started to blur and I could no longer focus. Finally, the pain forced me to close my eyes. I tied the security rope on the tree around my waist and back, and sat down on a nearby branch, feeling frightened and not knowing what was happening to me.

"I can't move, or see the floor," I shouted on the top of my voice.

"Yea, yea, you are afraid to go any higher," David shouted back.

"I can't see, I can't see," I kept repeating over and over, fright now clearly showing in the tone of my voice.

"Come on down," shouted Brian, gesticulating with both hands, instructing me to come down and stop messing about.

"I am not joking, honest; my side is hurting, really hurting, I can't move my legs, or see the ground. Get me down. Please, get me down. I'm afraid. Get me down, or I will fall." These were the only words I was able to speak.

"Stay where you are. Just stay and I will be with you in a minute," Gerald shouted, and he started to climb

"I feel dizzy and faint," I replied. "Help me, please, help."

David and Brian realised that my predicament was a serious matter. They started to climb the tree, directly behind Gerald. Matters were now serious. A fall from where I was sitting, high in the tree, could be life-threatening; they needed to get to me quickly, in case I became unconscious and let go.

"Wrap the rope round you," David shouted. "Can you hear me? Tie the rope around you, and do it now, quickly."

I tied the rope tightly round my back and hands, unable to see if it was secure because my body had started to bend into a ball. I had never felt such pain before, and knew something was seriously wrong with me. I could hear shouts from below but could not make out who was shouting. All sounds seemed to be merging into one and I felt myself starting to lose unconsciousness.

"Hold on, hold on," the three of them were shouting. I was shaking my head from side to side, desperately trying to stay awake. Gerald was the first to reach me, followed by David, with Brian behind. By this time, I was only semiconscious and could not make out the faces of my friends.

"Stay awake, stay awake," was all I could understand. I felt Gerald and David leaning against me, to stop me falling from the branch.

"Is he all right? Brian was below them, manoeuvring himself underneath the branch I was sitting on, trying to hold my feet.

I was in a difficult situation, near the top of a tree, unable to move, barely conscious, in constant pain, and with three people trying to stop me falling to the ground. The main problem was how to get me safely down. I clearly could not climb down.

"Get the rope from the swing on the branch above you, David," Brian instructed, looking up at the three of us.

"Yes, pass the rope and tie it around him, so that we can lower him to the ground," Gerald agreed.

"Will it be long enough to reach the floor?" David enquired.

"No, but it will reach that branch lower down, and we can easily hand him down to the ground from there," Brian said, pointing at a protruding branch below him.

The rope was tied under my arms, and I was slowly lowered onto this branch, and then brought to the ground and safety. I lay on the forest floor, in constant pain, but glad to be under the tree, not at the top, in its branches. The firm turf under my body had never felt so good. The three of them stood over me, feeling relieved that I was safe, and congratulating themselves on a job well done. I was glad, too, that the job was done. I looked up and then fell unconscious.

The next thing I remember is waking up under the bed

sheets, in my house. The three of them had carried me as far as the pit surface, and a few of the men, seeing the situation, ran to help, and carried me the rest of the way home. The doctor was immediately called and a few injections were administered. I was instructed to stay in bed and sleep, and he said that he would call back the following day, to conduct a full examination when I was more fully awake.

Early the following morning, the doctor was back, this time with another doctor, who had come from the hospital. They both examined me fully, had a few words with my parents, and I was told that an ambulance was on its way to take me to hospital.

"What is wrong with me, dad?" I was feeling nervous about going into hospital.

"You have a rotten appendix, and they need to take a look at your side," he replied, trying to smile and not look in the slightest worried.

"What does that mean? Will I need an operation?" I asked.

"The hospital will know what is best, and we will all be with you, so don't worry, everything is going to be all right. They will know how to fix the pain in your side. Just you wait and see," he assured me, smiling and trying to make light of the whole situation.

"When you were in hospital, daddy, you nearly died, and we were all frightened. What will happen to me?" I was starting to cry as I spoke these words.

"When I was in hospital, it was for a rest. I wish they would let me swap places with you! I could do with a few days off work. As for all this talk of dying and being frightened, the only thing you need to worry about is all the work that will be waiting for you in the garden when you come back home. Don't you think for one minute, side ache or no side ache, that you are getting out of these chores. They will all be waiting for you, so, if I were you, I would stay in hospital as long as you are able."

These words were spoken while he was laughing, pretending to scold me for skiving off to the hospital. It was my father's way, to try and make a joke of the whole situation, and not to show that he, too, was worried.

Less than half an hour later, the ambulance arrived and I was taken into hospital. After being pulled this way and that way, turned up, turned over, prodded here and prodded there, it was decided that I needed an appendectomy. The operation was to take place that night, because the appendix was gangrenous and, if it burst, the poison would travel quickly all over my body, and kill me in a matter of hours.

All my stomach and part of my back were painted in a yellow coloured sterilizing liquid that smelled of antiseptic. It had that distinctive hospital smell. No one can describe it exactly, but everyone can recognise it. With your eyes shut, you would not need to be told you were entering a hospital. When the preparations were complete, I was ready for surgery. My father and mother were at my side while a pre-med injection was administered, before I was taken to the operating theatre. I remember looking at the nurse and my parents, and being moved onto another trolley by a porter. I felt my eyelids grow heavy, and then I lost consciousness.

I lost all track of time and had no idea how long the operation lasted. I remember seeing lights everywhere and hearing voices in the background. The other thing I remember is a feeling of falling ever downward, trapped in a spiral. I could hear my parents talking to me but their voices seemed to be unreal and a long way away, as if they were in another room. I was drifting between consciousness and unconsciousness, between substance and air, between solid and space, between this world and the next. It was a strange experience, as if I no were no longer part of the real world, but drifting in empty space.

At one end of this emptiness I could see a light, drawing me forward into the unknown world of the dead. I was spinning in a vacuum, totally out of control, as the power of this light drew me on. I was in no man's land, on a sea with no anchor. I was a bottle drifting on the surface of the water, with my soul trapped inside, and tossed between the two worlds, the living and the dead.

The drifting sensation started to slow down, and I felt myself move away from the light and back into my body. I felt the solidness of the bed beneath by back and air in my lungs. The distant sounds were becoming nearer. I awoke to the smiles of my parents, one to each side of the bed. I could not see them at first, but knew it was my parents by the sounds of their voices. After a while, their loving faces began to move from haze to clarity. I could now focus clearly. A nurse lifted up my head and made me take a drink of water.

"How are you feeling?" my father asked, a broad smile on his face.

"I don't know. I feel tired and giddy, and I was falling into a large hole."

"We nearly lost you for a while there, but you should be all right now," the nurse told me, smiling at me, still holding up my head. She made me take another drink.

"You gave us quite a shock there, for a while, boy," my father said.

"Don't do that again. You had us all worried," my mother added, pointing her finger at me and laughing, as if I had a choice in the matter. I did not realise it at the time, but I had been on the threshold of death, and he did not let me in, but sent me back home to wait for another day.

Recovery after the operation was quick. Within a few days, I was sitting up in bed; a few days after that, I was able to walk, slowly and unsteadily, to the toilet at the end of the ward. My side was still painful, but it was not the sharp pain. There was a muted, throbbing pain, and, as the wound healed, it started to itch. I was still unable to stretch or move suddenly, because of the stitches in my side, but I was getting stronger by the hour and looking forward to coming out of hospital.

Visiting times were from six to eight every evening, and there were always several visitors around my bed. The side table by the bed was piled high with sweets, chocolates and fresh fruit. I was making the most of this enforced hospitalisation, and asked for comics and extra pocket money. I had the comics but not the money, although it was worth a try. Mog was a regular visitor and, after he left, there would always be a few shillings left on the side table, which I quickly placed into my wallet, in case they caught cold.

They informed me that the stitches would be taken out on the following day and, if everything went well, I would be home within a few days. The stitches came out, and the next day, I was sent home. The ambulance arrived just after mid afternoon, picking up four people and me. The last one to be dropped off was me.

In hospital, I had felt fine and full of life but, for the first few days at home, I felt tired and lethargic. It would be some weeks before I would be able to resume my normal schedule.

Chapter 35

THE GANG VISITED OUR HOUSE regularly, and used to bring a few packets of crisps that we consumed together. Pat also called, to see how I was progressing, and said she was looking forward to me coming to tea. She gave me a kiss on the cheek. I was not looking forward to meeting her parents: the gossip about them among the gang was not good. They said her father would ask me all types of questions, and I did not relish this one bit, but, where needs must, I will follow, and be on my best behaviour.

For the next few weeks I was housebound, unable to walk for more than five minutes at a time. Gradually, I started to feel better and began to take short walks in the garden, with my father or Mog, staying out a little longer on each occasion. It was not long before I regained full strength and was back to almost complete health. I was able to walk and run again, and the gang was back together once more. We all met one night at Brian's house, to decide what we would do for the rest of the summer, and discuss how I should handle the invitation to tea with Pat.

The only one who had a girlfriend was Kevin, and we all wished to know how he was able to manage that, when we were having difficulty. She combed his hair, and he smiled like a Cheshire cat when she was fussing over him, both of them laughing and joking together.

"When did you ask her to be your girlfriend?" I asked, thinking that, perhaps, he was not as half soaked as we all thought.

"A few weeks ago, I offered to share half my bar of chocolate with her if she would become my girlfriend," he replied.

"You mean, she said yes straight away! What about her parents?" I asked in astonishment.

"What about her parents? It's the daughter I am courting, not the parents."

I looked at him in bewilderment. There was nothing more to be said after this, and so I changed the subject from her parents back to her. "Have you kissed her yet?"

"Of course I have. That is what you do with girlfriends," he told me.

"Did you ask her first, or just kiss her," I asked.

"Neither. She kissed me, and showed me how to tongue-kiss," he added, smiling.

This made me really envious. I had never really kissed any girl, let alone tongue-kissed. My father's words were right, when he said the girl catches you, not the other way about. It was obvious that she knew more than Kevin, and when she threw out her hook, Kevin swallowed the bait whole.

"How do you tongue-kiss, Kev?" I asked, never having heard of this new way to kiss.

"That is easy. You just kiss, touching tongues," he replied.

"I knew that!" I felt disgusted to think that anyone could kiss with an open mouth.

The following week, Sunday afternoon, was the time for the tea with Pat's parents. I was to call at her house at four o'clock, and started to dread the very moment. The day arrived. That morning, I debated with my father about what I should wear, and how I should behave.

"A clean white shirt, smart long trousers, with a coat. Make sure you clean your shoes; there is nothing worse than dirty shoes. It shows you could not be bothered to make an effort," he advised.

"I'll get a hair cut this morning, and make sure my hair is neat and tidy."

"That is a good idea. Call into Mrs Adams, too, and buy a

box of chocolates for her mother," he suggested, handing me the money to pay for the purchase.

Mrs. Adams' shop was one small room in the front of a house: the parlour turned into a shop. The far wall of the room was covered with shelves, which were filled with jars of different sweets, all neatly stacked in rows. The other side of the wall was covered in tins and jars, all stacked in different sections and clearly labelled.

A wooden counter went through the centre of the room, its top covered with small cardboard boxes, all arranged next to one another and filled with different types of sweets, which were sold singly, or in twos and threes. Under the window were various boxes of chocolates and packed sweets, stacked on top of each other in an untidy heap. The whole shop had a dilapidated look about it, and a lot of old tins and boxes occupied any available space.

Mrs. Adams was in her seventies, short, stout and very rounded. She always wore an apron that came down to the floor; a hair net covered the whole of her head. Her hands and face were grubby, and her clothes looked as if they and she were in permanent need of a wash.

You entered the shop by the front door, and waited in the passage, after you had knocked the side door, for her to come out from the back of the house. A while later, she would appear, carrying a large key. The shop door would be opened and we would enter.

"Could I have a box of chocolates, please, Mrs. Adams?"

She walked over to the side of the window, picked up a few boxes and asked which one I wanted. I chose to the smallest one, assuming that it would be the cheapest.

The side and back of the shop were alive with chickens, clucking and shuffling about on the floor, one even jumped up on the counter, as if he wished to be served next. I gesticulated to Mrs. Adams, who had other customers and it did not look as if they intended to pay. When she saw the chicken on the counter and all the other chickens, she started to wave her hands into the air and flap her head one way and the other in startled alarm, and shouted,"The chickens are out, the chickens have escaped, close the front door."

I slammed the front door, although this did not seem right to me. The chickens must have come into the shop from the outside, so why did Mrs. Adams bellow at me to close the door? The sharpness in her voice meant that I did not argue, just followed the instruction given. I returned, after closing the door, half expecting to go back to the front door, to reopen it and chase the chickens out of shop and house. A few of the chickens were now moving upstairs to the bedrooms, and there was quite a commotion when Mrs. Adams started to chase them around the shop.

"Catch them, block them off, check all hiding places, they have done this before," Mrs. Adams cried.

Done what before? They should not be in the house. "Shall I open the door and let them out," I asked.

Mrs. Adams was spitting and shouting. I was glad the chocolates were in a box and covered. "Let them out! Let them bloody out! They have not been out since they were born; they don't know what out means." She caught one of the chickens by the wing, took it by the neck, looked into its eyes and said, "Sylvester, this is your fault. You are the boss and, if you try to escape again, your head is coming off, do you hear me? Coming off!" She shook the poor chicken's head violently.

"Where did they all come from, if not from outside," I asked, totally confused.

"From under the table. They belong under the table, they were born under the table, and they should stay under the table, and back under the bloody table they will go," she shouted, running to catch another chicken. "Don't just stand there. Catch a few and throw them under the table," she shouted at me.

"Hurry up; hurry up, before they hide."

The door into the back of the house was wide open and I saw a large table in the middle of the room, its legs all covered in small wire mesh, which had been wrapped around the outside of the table legs and ran the length of the table. The whole of the underside of the table was a chicken coop. In the centre of the table was a large, round hole, which I later learned was a feeding hole for the chickens. All waste from the table was channelled down this hole, to feed the occupants below. The top of the table was covered with plates of various sizes, saucepans, jars, a teapot, and a number of other implements that I did not recognize.

A bowl of potato peelings, some cabbage leaves, and a few carrots, well past their sell-by date, were all on one corner of the table, waiting to be fed later to the chickens. On the other corner of the table were two loaves of bread, one with mould on the top, a pile of old crusts and a few squashed pieces of cake, also awaiting the hole.

The chickens were all over the house by now; a few were up on the counter, pecking at the sweets. Mrs. Adams was having an apoplectic fit, spitting with rage at the audacity of the birds. "Get off, get off the counter, leave the sweets alone, you must pay for them first, sweets are not free, shoo, shoo, get down, you wicked creatures," she was shouting, her face full of red-hot anger.

She was running from one side of the shop to the other, kicking out and shouting at the chickens to get out of the shop and leave the sweets alone. "Wicked birds! Birds from hell! They're all going in the pot. I'll boil the buggers alive. Sweets are to be sold and paid for, not gobbled up by chickens."

She grabbed another bird, rushed into the other room and threw it under the wire mesh around the table. She adjusted the mesh, to stop the chicken from escaping again. I grabbed two chickens off the counter, just as one of them decided to mark the area by using its bottom, missing my hand but firmly establishing its territory as the mess splashed all over the sweets. Mrs. Adams would expect payment, and I did not rate the chicken's chances of remaining alive for another day, if the money were not forthcoming immediately. I carried the two chickens into the next room and placed them under the wire and out of harms way.

Twenty minutes later, all the chickens were safely under the table, inside the wire, and looking none the worse for their ordeal. The same could not be said for Mrs. Adams. Her hair net was half over her head, hair hanging in all directions. Her face was blood red on one side; the other side was black from crawling under the counter. The front of her apron was covered in feathers and her clothes dishevelled.

She rubbed her hands over her apron, placed her hair under her net, emptied the peelings and the bread down the hole, clenched her fists towards the hole, as if practising ringing the chickens' necks, and slowly regained her composure. She adjusted her clothes and brushed the feathers off her front. She then went back into the shop, with me following behind, still in disbelief at what had just happened. I was thanked for helping her catch the chickens, and handed a few sweets as my reward. As I started to walk to the front door, she shouted at me to leave it open on my way out.

A few seconds later, I was out on the pavement, a bag of sweets in one hand and chocolates in the other, bemused and incredulous to think that chickens were kept under the table in the house. It was quite common for chickens to be kept in the back garden and left to roam in the lane, but to keep chickens in the house, as part of the family, was a new one on me. I would not have believed it if I had not witnessed it with my own eyes.

I looked down at my trousers and shoes, and they were stained with chicken mess. There were long, white and brown streaks down both trouser legs and over my shoes. I was literally covered with the stuff, and was expected at Pat's house in a few minutes. I could feel my temperature rising at the thought of her father asking me why my trousers and shoes were dirty. I did not have time to go home and change. Pat had already emphasized the importance of being punctual. Her parents could not stand bad time-keeping. They looked on it as a lack of respect, and that is the last impression I wanted to give, on the first visit.

I called on Brian, who lived a few doors down from the shop, and asked if he could help. After he had been laughing for a few minutes, and holding his nose, and doing all he could to make me feel foolish, his mother appeared, dabbed me down with a wet sponge, cleaned my shoes with a wet cloth, and left me looking presentable again. Brian started tormenting me again, and doing his best to make me feel foolish. I just smiled at him. It was useless to ask him to leave me alone.

"If you stop calling me smelly chicken poo and laughing, I will give you my sweets." I tried to look all dejected and pretended to be conquered.

"I want the whole bag," he demanded, "and I won't call you names and laugh any more, or tell the gang."

"You win," I replied, looking sad and beaten, and handed him the sweets given to me by Mrs. Adams. I turned around, to hide my large grin. I knew where these sweets had been. The last laugh is on me, I thought, and went on my way. I had only had chicken mess on my clothes and shoes; he would soon have it in his mouth, after he had eaten the sweets I had just handed over. The chicken had clearly marked these sweets, when it was on the counter, or Mrs. Adams would not have let me have them free of charge.

A few minutes later, I arrived at Pat's parents' house and knocked the door. The door opened and it was Pat.

"Come on in. We are expecting you. Tea is all ready," she said, talking in a sharp, businesslike tone, and inviting me into the front room by pointing me in the general direction. I felt like a little lamb being led to the slaughter. Why do we go through this pain and humiliation? They say that if there is no pain there is no gain. The trouble is, I was too young to know what *the gain* would be, but did recognize it was worth the pain, and knew that each of these steps brought me nearer to that mysterious gain.

"Nice to meet you, Mr. Griffith." I held out my hand to Pat's father. He shook it hard and asked me to be seated. Mrs. Griffith entered the room, smiling at me as she sat down, immediately placing me at ease.

"I have known your father for years. How is he?"

"Very well. He is busy in the garden at this time of year, in between his shifts at the pit, Mr. Griffith, sir," I replied, starting now to get over the nervous feeling I was experiencing when at the front door.

"We have jelly and blancmange, with fresh bread and butter for tea, followed by ham and cheese sandwiches and lemonade," Mrs. Griffith said. Pat sat down beside her, on the arm on the chair.

"Jelly and blancmange are my favourites, as well as ham and cheese sandwiches. You should not have gone to all this trouble," I replied. "It is very kind of you, thank you."

"No trouble. This is our regular Sunday treat, and we are glad you could join us," she replied.

Mr. Griffith sat quietly in the chair, watching me closely. "You're a bit of a smooth one, a tad over polite, if you ask me," he remarked, trying to weigh me up. "You like my daughter, then? She is a fine girl," he remarked, slightly closing his eyes and looking from his wife to me. I felt he was on to me.

I replied, "Pat is very considerate and, yes, I like her company."

"As long as that is all you want, we will get along fine, really fine," he announced.

His wife chastised him for being over forward, and Pat sat blushing next to her mother, dangling her legs back and forth.

"These are for you, Mrs. Griffith." I handed her the chocolates.

"There is no need for these," she replied, smiling.

"I insist. I have been saving my pocket money, so here, please take them. Pat has told me so many good things about you." I had not meant to say that. She might think her daughter had been talking about her, and she could be annoyed. My fear was groundless. She gracefully accepted the gift. If she knew what I was after, she would not be so happy, I thought.

It was less than an hour since my father gave me the money, and it was his idea, not mine, to buy chocolates, but the credit belonged to me. I was sure he would not mind me telling a little white lie and taking all the credit, if he knew the precarious situation I was encountering. I needed all the ammunition I could muster, to get on the right side of Mr. Griffith.

"Thank you. It is very kind of you and shows what a thoughtful young man you are. I will enjoy them when listening to the radio," she replied, smiling at me. She placed the box of chocolates on the opposite arm of the chair from where her daughter was sitting. I also noticed Pat looking at me in appreciation of my thoughtful ways. I was definitely making an impression. I just needed a smile from Mr. Griffith and I would be there, but when I looked over at him, he was still stony-faced.

The meal went by very pleasantly. Mr. Griffith did not say a lot.

"The jelly and blancmange were just to my liking, Mrs. Griffith."

"All jelly is the same; one is the same as another," Mr. Griffith said grouchily.

"I meant to say red jelly is my favourite colour," I answered, trying desperately not to disagree with any thing he was saying.

"If you say so," he grunted.

"Would you like another sandwich?" Pat handed me the sandwich plate.

"No, thank you, I am full." I replied politely.

Mr. Griffith looked at me for a few moments and snapped at me in a sharp voice, "How do you expect to grow big and strong, if you don't eat? Have another sandwich; there are plenty left."

"Thank you, I will have another cheese one, if I'm allowed." I took the sandwich and put it on my plate, still trying to be as polite as possible.

"Have you any hobbies, besides chasing girls," he asked.

This question had me floored for a while, and my colour started to rise. I must say something positive; his voice denoted disapproval of chasing girls.

"No, I haven't the time, or the inclination, to chase girls. Most of my time is spent with my ferrets and helping my father in the garden." This was the only answer I could think of.

"You have ferrets?" He had a sparkle in his eyes.

"Yes, and I intend to obtain a few more over the next few months."

Mr. Griffith told me, "I have a few ferrets in the back, and one polecat."

I perked up. "That is brilliant. I intend to obtain a polecat in the next few weeks."

Mr. Griffith sat up, looked at me and was just about to speak, when I added quickly, "I would very much like to see your ferrets, some time, when you are available." There was no pretence about it. We had found a common bond.

"What about now? Have you finished your food?"

"Finished and eager. I am ready." I stood up. We walked out into the back yard and into a shed, half way down the garden. Inside the shed were various hutches, standing on top of each other, and there was a ferret run on the end of the shed. As we entered, the ferrets were alert and pacing up and down with excitement.

Mr. Griffith opened the hutch, pulled out two ferrets and handed them to me. I was totally at ease in handling these creatures. I eagerly placed my hands around their necks and looked at their teeth. The ferrets I were holding were large, white ones, with a slight tinge of grey over their backs.

"Are they from the same litter, they look very similar?" I tipped them both up to examine the underside of their stomachs.

Mr. Griffith looked approvingly at the way I handled these creatures, and replied, "They are just over a year old and sisters. Their mother and father are there." He pointed to a large hutch under the shed window. I handed ferrets back and asked him if one of them was pregnant.

"Yes, you're a sharp one. The father is in the bottom cage," he replied, pointing to a large white ferret.

"Perhaps I could breed from my ferret as well. I could bring her down and place her in the cage with the male for a few days. He looks in fine shape." I had lost all inhibition when on the subject of ferrets. "You could have the pick of the litter, if that would be acceptable." Things were taking a turn for the better.

"No, I have enough ferrets, but I would be only too pleased to help. Bring your ferret down next weekend, and we will give it a try."

"Thank you, Mr Griffith."

He showed me the rest of his ferrets.

We must have been in the shed for over half an hour and would have stayed longer if Mrs Griffith had not shouted at us to come and have a cup of tea. We returned to the house, and I sat next to Pat.

Mr Griffith said, "The lad is welcome here, any time. He is a good lad, knows all about ferrets." He was speaking to his wife but looking at me.

I had broken the ice with Mr. Griffith and felt that he was

now on my side; if not totally happy about thinking of me with his daughter, at least he was relaxed about our shared interest in ferret-keeping and -breeding. I was definitely making an impression and found myself in his good books, where I intended to stay. I thanked them both for the tea. Pat walked me to the door and waved me goodbye.

A few days later, the five of us met at Kevin's house, to advance our knowledge of courting. I already had my first real date and needed to know a lot more about this courting business.

"What do you talk about when you are with your girlfriend, Kev?"

"We don't talk," he replied.

"If you don't talk, what do you do?"

"We kiss." He laughed.

This made us all really envious. I did not even touch Pat's hand on my date, let alone kiss her.

"How do you go about kissing?" Deadeye probed, looking at me as if to say, "we need to hone our hunting skills to kissing skills. Kissing is more fun."

David, wishing desperately to partake of the kissing action, asked, "How do you do it, Kev?"

"Do what?"

"Get the girls to like you."

"I tell them stories and tell them they are beautiful," Kevin explained.

Deadeye tut-tutted and said, "I am not telling them they are beautiful, or any stories; they are girls." He thought for a moment, and added, "I could tell them stories of my hunting skills. What do you think?"

"I don't think they will be interested in hunting and things like that," I replied.

Kevin was the centre of attention and enjoying every minute of it. For once, we were all listening to him, and asking him questions about his courting and kissing skills, and he was making the most of his moment of glory. All the girls liked Kevin, even Pat. On my first real date, she had commented about Kevin, "He is really cool."

We all wished to be 'cool', and my next question to Kevin, thinking about Pat's comments, were, "How do you be *cool*, Kev?"

"Be funky and fab," he responded.

Kevin was forever grooming himself and combing his hair, which had now grown back. He washed it everyday, sometimes twice a day, if he wanted to be doubly funky and fab. Our parents would have to drag us to the sink to wash face and hands, let alone wash our hair twice a day.

"All this funking and fabbing is not on!" Deadeye remarked. "I am fabbing no one, or funking any girl."

"I don't mind a bit of funking about, if it means I can start courting," Gerald remarked, with a large smile on his face. I was already courting and felt a little more advanced then the rest of the gang, but not in Kevin's league.

"I am courting but have not done any funking yet. Perhaps I should have been funking and fabbing first with Pat, and then started to court her," I said, looking at Kevin for an answer. He did not reply, but just looked at us all, as if to say, you don't have a clue.

That night, walking home down the hill from Vicarage Terrace, I was thinking about how we were all getting older, and wondering what the future would hold, and realising how life was changing for us. The pits were in full swing. There were those who claimed that coal was no longer profitable and things would need to change, but no one took any notice of such things. We had heard these stories before, and paid very little attention to newspaper reports. We expected life to go on for us in very much in the same way as it had done for our parents and their parents before them. The only change we expected was that from childhood into adulthood, and we were all looking forward to growing up and carving out a place for ourselves in the Valley.

We had little idea of the extent to which things were to change in the coming decade. The old ways were about to end forever. The changes would be dramatic and painful. We were growing into young men; the adults were about to lose their jobs. Turmoil and strife were around the corner, and unemployment about to become the norm. Black Gold was to lose its supremacy. Its rule was almost at an end, its power on the verge of being broken.

The mountains of slag were to be transformed, the Black Hole was to be filled in forever and become a memory of how things used to be. The two obnoxious objects were to be demolished, and the competition between them about to come to an end; boys, men and mountains of the Valley were about to change forever, but that is another story.

dinas

For more information about this innovative imprint,
contact Lefi Gruffudd at lefi@ylolfa.com or go to
www.ylolfa.com/dinas.
A Dinas catalogue is also available.